A Guide to Liberating Your Soul

◆◆◆

Richard Barrett

Fulfilling Books

Published by
Fulfilling Books
P.O. Box 19926, Alexandria, VA 22320

Publisher's Cataloging in Publication Data:
Barrett, Richard, 1945-
    A Guide to Liberating Your Soul.
    Includes index, illustrations and bibliography.
    1. Spirituality. 2. Consciousness. 3. Transpersonal Psychology
    ISBN 0-9643226-3-3
    Preassigned LCCN: 95-90452
    Softcover.
    First edition.

Cover design by May Eidi.
Photograph by Susan D. Coronis.
Manufactured in the United States of America.
First printing, July 1995.

For Nancy, Chris,
and my mother and father.

Acknowledgments

This book came into being through the encouragement of many people:

Nancy, my wife, and Chris, our son, whose love, support, and understanding allowed me the freedom to embrace my dreams.

My editor, Sarwat Hussain, who challenged me to become more than I was, and to live up to my highest expectations.

My friends, Wim Ahlers, Bill Bauman, Julius Hankin, and Martin Rutte, who believed in me and offered me unconditional support and encouragement on my journey.

My friend, David Gershon, who taught me the art of empowerment so that I could implement my vision.

My friend, Eli Bay, who lovingly shared with me his unpublished compilation of spiritual quotes entitled *The Meaningful Life: Spiritual Wisdom to Inspire the Seeker.* The quotes at the beginning of each chapter are taken from Eli's compilation.

Members of the Association for Research and Enlightenment study group that met at our home for four years and gave me feedback during the formative stages of my writing.

Members of the World Bank's Spiritual Unfoldment Society, who had the courage to join me in bringing spirituality into our work place.

My friends, Karon Brashares and Vicki Worthington, whose constructive comments helped polish the final draft.

I am deeply grateful to all of you.

Contents

Part Two: Transformation

Preface
A Vision

On a November evening in 1991, I had a vision. I was sitting on the veranda of a cottage in the foothills of Mt. Kenya. I had spent most of the afternoon working on an early draft of this book, and had taken a moment to contemplate the beauty of the garden before me. Almost without a perceptible change in consciousness a vision appeared to me.

It was a vision of the world where good and evil and heaven and hell had dissolved into understanding. There was no right or wrong. Justice took care of itself through the ebb and flow of a dynamic harmony of cause and effect. In this world of love and abundance every unconscious desire was taken care of in anticipation of the need. Doors opened where none had existed, and the content of shadows was revealed in light. Jealousy and hatred had no meaning in this vision.

I felt a sense of detachment from every aspect of the culture and society that I had once embraced. At the center of that detachment was unity at the grandest scale. This was a feeling of oneness with every aspect of my surroundings. It was not a lonely feeling, it was as if I were a single cell, surrounded by a multitude of other cells, all of which formed part of a living being with love coursing through its veins. Every other cell was as special and unique as myself. We each had our contribution to make to the life of the body. Just as the body was dependent on us, so were we dependent on it. The vitality of every cell contributed to the well being of the whole. By fulfilling my mission and supporting other cells, I was contributing to the health of the whole.

As this vision took hold of my consciousness, I felt a sense of power flooding through my mind. This was the same power that flows through a drop of water when it forms part of an ocean wave. It was, at the same time, mine and yet not mine. Mine because I could feel it flowing through me. Not mine because I knew it came from the whole. I felt fulfilled and complete in every respect with no fear for the future, nor regret for the past. The future and the past existed only in my beliefs. They had no reality other than that which I gave them. I could transform them to be whatever I wanted them to be, and I could change them into something else. I was sure and certain of every aspect of my life because it was all rooted in the present.

The fear had gone out of living. All I had to do was choose my destination. I say choose, but there was no choice as such. I simply followed my intuition and allowed my inner desires to express themselves. No logic was necessary, just a sense of flowing with the current of an ocean. By allowing my intuition to rule, I did not have to worry about getting to my destination. I did not need to be proactive in deciding the route. As long as I kept the vision of my destination clear, the details took care of themselves. As soon as I created a goal, it was as if the result already existed. I simply walked in its direction to make it appear. Although obstacles arose, they were not impediments. As soon as I recognized that impediments were of my own invention, they disappeared. They did not have a life of their own. Their only strength was the strength I gave them. It was the same with sickness and suffering. They too derived their strength from my belief in them. Through the recognition that they were a product of my creation they became malleable and lost their strength.

At that moment I realized that this knowledge of the mind's supremacy could revolutionize the world. Through its systematic teaching and application, a new generation would be born that could live without fear, in abundance and peace. No longer would we turn to drugs to cure the sick. Suffering could be cured through mind healing. Medicine based on drugs would become the medicine of last resort. Crime and every other expression of anger would be recognized as a product of self-manufactured fear. The practice of mind healing would be pervasive throughout society. Mind health would be taught at all levels in our educational systems. Psycho-spiritual counselors would become the teachers of the future. Their profession would be based upon the unifying principles of psychology, religion and science.

That vision set the seal on the direction that my research for this book would take. What follows is the result. Part One explores the world of beliefs and the concept of spirituality and develops a model of reality based on consciousness that draws together contemporary theories of psychology, religion and science. Part one also explains the interactions of the personality and the soul. Part Two gives practical guidance on liberating your soul, provides examples of spiritual unfoldment drawn from real life experiences and sets out strategies for attuning your personality with your soul.

Imagine you are a masterpiece unfolding, every second of every day—a work of art taking form with every breath.
Thomas Crum

The whole purpose of spiritual unfoldment is for the individual man to train himself so that he becomes a more powerful cache from which the love of God can radiate. Grace Cook

What the spiritual path offers is a way to come back into balance, to develop our intuition and the wisdom of the heart, so that the intellect is no longer the master, but instead is the servant of our heart, the part of us that brings us into unity with ourselves and all other beings. Ram Dass

A man must first find his own soul. He who has found and knows his soul has found all the worlds, has achieved all his desires. The Upanishads

Introduction
A Personal Journey

The journey we call life is the process that leads to the unfoldment of the soul. It can be a voyage of personal transformation, or it can seem like an unending, meaningless struggle. It is your choice. If you choose the path of personal transformation, you embark on a life-changing mission to bring your personality into alignment with your soul. The benefits that accompany this attunement include more honest and responsive relationships, heightened creativity, enhanced health and well-being, a sense of abundance, feelings of inner joy and peace, and reduced stress. You begin to sense an inner connection with the very core of your being. Life becomes full of meaning as your personality blends with your soul.

The process of transformation is like the unfolding of a flower. Just as buds unfold to reveal the full beauty of the flower, so does your personality unfold to reveal the beauty of your soul. As you release your fears and embrace unconditional love, you uncover your soul. The time required depends on you. The more you are committed to personal transformation and a willingness to face your fears, the more rapid your progress—the process of unfoldment is driven by your intention and application. It is all up to you. While others can provide you with insights and facilitate your process, only you can uncover your soul. Just as the flower fulfills its destiny by blooming, so, too, do you fulfill your destiny by liberating your soul.

The journey of unfoldment begins by developing an understanding of who "you" are. "Know thyself" has been one of the principal teachings of religious philosophers through the ages. Through self-knowledge you tap into the intuition and wisdom that exist in the fourth dimension of human consciousness. As you begin to recognize your soul nature and make contact with your multi-dimensional consciousness, you find your sense of self expanding. When you begin to identify with your soul self, the barriers that prevented open communication and cooperation with your family, friends, and colleagues disappear. Your life and your relationships take on new meaning. The door to a new future begins to open.

The keys that open the door to this new future are not to be found in the external world. They have nothing to do with wealth, status, or education. They are simply your beliefs. Beliefs are the frameworks around which we construct our reality. By changing your beliefs you can change your reality. Beliefs can be strongly rooted or transient, and they can be conscious or unconscious. When you fully understand the importance of your beliefs, you will want to create your reality consciously. You will want to be fully in control of the creative power of your mind. To do this, you must bring into the light the beliefs that lie in the shadows of the unconscious. As you become aware of your unconscious beliefs, you begin to understand the impact they have on your life.

You will discover that your emotional pain and suffering are caused by fear-laden beliefs and your fears are simply memories of past pain projected into the future. By bringing your unconscious negative beliefs into your conscious awareness and releasing them, you give yourself the space to envision a different future—a future without emotional pain. Your beliefs give strength to your memories. If you can change your belief about the meaning of what happened in the past, then you can change your future. Every moment in your life is a chance to begin anew, a chance to choose love over fear. Love allows you to grow and evolve. Fear causes you to contract and withdraw from life.

Emotional discomfort and pain occur when fear beliefs are held at some level of your consciousness. They arise because of the imbalance between the energy of love in your soul and the energy of fear in your personality. The discomfort you feel is an energy imbalance due to the lack of attunement of your personality with your soul. The more you are out of alignment, the more pain and discomfort you encounter in your life. If you consistently ignore or hide your emotional discomfort, the negative energy accumulates and eventually manifests in your body as sickness or disease.

Emotional discomfort and pain, when properly understood, are positive signals alerting you to wrong thinking and guiding you to right thinking. As you release the fears that surround your personality, you improve your alignment with your soul. This is the process and the promise of spiritual unfoldment. The promise manifests itself as your personality and your soul become fully integrated. You will no longer be a human "being," you will become a soul, experiencing life as a human being.

By accepting the challenge to live as a soul, you embark on a life-changing mission. The difficulties you encounter will be small in comparison to the rewards. Soul-living requires us to be fearless, disciplined, and, above all caring—for ourselves and for others. We learn that the energy we put out into the world is the energy we get back. As you embrace your soul, you acquire a new identity—an identity that is larger and more inclusive than you could have possibly imagined. You find a new sense of meaning and purpose in life. Your intuition grows and you reach new heights of creativity. This is the promise of spiritual unfoldment.

Part One
Self-knowledge

The kingdom of heaven is within you, and whosoever shall know himself shall find it. Jesus Christ

The world view of physics, the insights of parapsychology, and the purview of mysticism are essentially the same: a universe of purposeful mind ever evolving its creation toward higher consciousness. Rolland Gammon

One has not only an ability to perceive the world but an ability to alter one's perception of it; more simply, one can change things by the manner in which one looks at them. Tom Robbins

There is no greater victory in the life of a human being than victory over the mind. Swami Ramadas

1

Models of Reality

A ll of us, either consciously or unconsciously, attempt to interpret our experiences in terms of a greater whole. Beginning in our early childhood, we each develop a personal model of reality based on our beliefs. Our models become the reference systems that influence our thoughts and actions and give structure and meaning to our experiences. Nearly all of our models contain a mixture of scientific, psychological, and religious beliefs.

When we encounter phenomena that fall outside the realm of our beliefs, we are faced with two choices: we can either accept the challenge of broadening our perspective to incorporate the new information, or revert to denial. Thus, for some, life's experiences broaden their understanding and their belief systems expand. Those with rigid belief filters find it difficult to accept new ideas, or different points of view. By seeing only what they want to see, they deny themselves the possibility of experiencing any reality other than that in which they believe. They force themselves into a cocoon of insecure comfort, shrink from life, and never attain their full potential.

Our evolving belief systems
The beliefs we use to construct our models of the world are simply the products of our environments and our life experiences. They are the road maps bequeathed to us by our parents, the society in which

we live, the religious traditions into which we were born, and our personal experiences. The beliefs we develop from our life experiences are mostly gained through the operation of the law of cause and effect in our lives. We quickly learn that fire burns. Electricity shocks and persistence pays off. We become particularly adept at dealing with the material world where the laws of cause and effect appear to work with some degree of predictability. This is the reason why we are all so enamored with science. Science delights in giving us rules and laws that lend credence to the belief systems about our three-dimensional physical world. We believe what science tells us because it predicts results with accuracy. For this reason science has become universally accepted. However, the domains to which the laws of science apply are limited.

First, science is almost exclusively applied to the external physical world. Scientists have been unwilling, or unable, to address the inner world of belief, emotion, and thought, and have rarely ventured to explain para-normal or meta-physical experiences. In short, science does not serve us well in understanding the nonphysical nature of the universe. Science, as it has been practiced to date, has largely ignored the role of consciousness.

Second, science focuses on linear systems. It reduces life's processes to their smallest parts and offers explanations that are then extrapolated to the larger world. In doing so science ignores the chaos of life and the spontaneity of organic systems. The holistic approach that considers the body, mind, and soul as a functioning interactive system is an anathema to scientists.

Despite the reductionism of science, it has served us well in many ways. Through science we have begun to understand our physical environment, and we have gained knowledge about how our bodies work. We are even now beginning to understand the linkages between the human mind and the human body. However, the knowledge that science has provided is relatively new. Up until the beginning of the 18th century, no western school or college taught science. Science as a discipline did not exist because of the strong influence the Church had over human belief systems.

From around 400 A.D. to the beginning of the 18th century every unexplainable aspect of our lives was subjected to a religious explanation. Mankind depended on its religious leaders to explain disasters, cure its sicknesses, and take care of its souls. The purveyors of religion held great power. Access to God was completely controlled by the Catholic Church and its clergy. The Pope could condemn a man to eternal damnation through excommunication. Immortality could only be assured by following catholic teachings. Because of this power, religious leaders held great sway. Kings, queens, and political leaders treated their spiritual intermediaries with caution and high regard. This period, which ended in the sixteenth century, was intolerant to belief systems that were not sanctioned by the Church of Rome. Other belief systems were considered heresy and other faiths as heathen. The Church ruled western belief systems absolutely.

Not surprisingly, free thinkers such as Martin Luther met with an accepting audience when they contested the spiritual and pastoral guidance of the Catholic Church. The challenge to the Church's intermediacy between humanity and God and the belief that God's forgiveness could be obtained freely and individually led to the reformation of Christianity.

At about this time science also began its struggle with the Church. The conflict began in the field of astronomy. In 1543, Nicholas Copernicus, a Polish Canon of the church, proposed that a rotating earth revolving around a stationary central sun could account for the movement of the heavens in a far simpler way than the theory of a central earth espoused by the Church. Copernicus' theory, which involved a radical reordering of beliefs about the nature of the universe, was later developed by Galileo in 1632. Since these theories were regarded as being in direct contradiction to the official interpretation of the Bible, they generated violent opposition from the Church. For this heresy, Galileo was sentenced to prison in 1633. His sentence was later commuted to house arrest. Not until 1992, 359 years later, did the Catholic Church admit they had made a mistake in condemning Galileo. The commission of inquiry ruled that the clerics who had judged Galileo were unable to comprehend a nonliteral reading of the Bible and had feared that Galileo's teachings would undermine Catholic tradition.

The development of the new astronomy was also taken up by Johannes Kepler, a mathematician to the Holy Roman Emperor, Rudolf II, early in the seventeenth century. Kepler developed mathematical relationships to expand and explain the astronomy of Copernicus. These men of science, and others such as William Harvey and Isaac Newton, started to erode the Church's grip on belief systems. Science began to be taught in universities around 1700. The physical environment became the domain of the scientist. The Church restricted itself to the domain of the soul. The 1200 year domination of belief systems by the Church came to an end. Scientists and explorers exposed the fallacies of many religious interpretations of our physical environment. Physicists and biologists took up the front ranks in the march for truth. As science and medicine developed, the hold of religion diminished. Science took upon itself the quest of determining the *how*, the *where* and the *when* of our physical existence. However, the *why* proved to be more elusive. By limiting the *why* to the human mind the "science" of psychology was created. Prior to modern times the *why* was the subject of religious interpretations. Although psychology is called the science of the mind, the founders of psychology did not have such a limited view since they took the name from the word psyche meaning soul. In reality, most psychiatrists have little concern for the souls of their patients. Their main focus is on helping the patient to cope with crises in relationships and in daily functions. They do so through a process built on scientific and medical principles.

Science, religion, and psychology
Thus, in the past few centuries, we have moved from a purely religious explanation of the world to a tripartite model—the physical explained by science, the spiritual explained by religion and the mental explained by psychology. We find ourselves requiring three different areas of knowledge to explain the experiences of body, mind, and soul. Depending on the nature of the problem we encounter, we rely on one of these three belief systems to offer an

explanation. If our body gets sick or our car breaks down, we rely on science and technology to explain the problem. If we are involved in a dysfunctional relationship, we turn to psychology for explanations, and when a loved one dies, we turn to religion for comfort and understanding.

One of the major problems with our three belief systems is that certain phenomena and experiences lie outside their boundaries of knowledge. For example, miracles can be explained neither by science nor by religion; synchronicity can be explained neither by psychology nor by science; and spirituality lies outside the belief systems of religion and psychology. In addition, the topic of metaphysics lies outside all three belief systems.

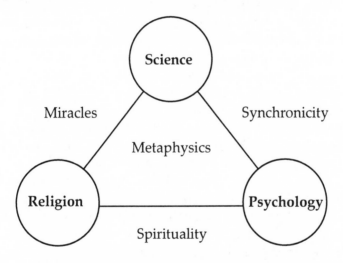

Figure 1: Boundaries of knowledge

Our modern world has accepted this fragmentation as a reality. Consequently we hand over responsibility for understanding our bodies, minds, and souls to "experts." We give up trying to find answers on our own. We delegate our responsibility for our own well-being to doctors, therapists, and priests. Only when we face life threatening situations do we turn to a personal God, as if deep down we know that beyond all fragmented knowledge lies a single cause.

Only when desperate do we turn to a belief system that has transcended time—a belief in a higher power that has dominion over life and death.

Within this century, there has been an increasing trend for specialists to relate their knowledge to other fields. There are psychologists, particularly those who embrace transpersonal theories, who are attempting to bring human mental states within a spiritual perspective. There are scientists, particularly those that embrace the ideas of modern physics, who are attempting to link science with the ideas of unity and God. There are also physicians who recognize the power of the mind over our physical bodies. Unfortunately, however, very few attempt to unify psychology, religion *and* science. The missing linkages become more conspicuous as the evidence from these three realms of inquiry begin to point in the direction of a single model.

The survival of the human species hinges on our ability to develop a holistic framework that recognizes the interrelatedness of all knowledge.

Increasingly it is becoming apparent that there is an explanation of our three-dimensional reality that embraces not only psychology, religion, and science, but metaphysics and mysticism.

This then begs the question: Why are attempts to develop such a model rare? The answer: An almost total acceptance of the reductionistic approach to research and learning. The structure of our learning institutions is such that research incentives favor vertical rather than lateral thinking. Anyone wishing to undertake holistic research must overcome significant institutional and funding barriers. But it is exactly this type of research and learning that we now need. We can no longer afford to ignore the significant interrelationships that exist between the different bodies of knowledge that make up our belief systems. The survival of the human species and the life forms that inhabit our planet hinges on our ability to develop a holistic framework that recognizes the interrelatedness of all knowledge.

The theory of quantum mechanics has turned the physical world into a lying, deceiving scoundrel and made our own five senses and central nervous systems into co-conspirators in an elaborate "reality sting," a fraud carried on successfully since time immemorial. Wes Nisker

Current concepts of the mind-brain relation involve a direct break with the long established materialist and behaviorist doctrine that has dominated neuroscience for many decades. Instead of renouncing or ignoring consciousness, the new interpretation gives full recognition to the primacy of inner conscious awareness as a causal reality. Roger Sperry

2

The Consciousness Model

This book proposes a unifying belief system that draws together scientific, religious, and psychological beliefs into a model of reality based on consciousness. We can only understand the principles that link these three realms of thought by recognizing the limits of our three-dimensional perception. The unifying theory involves concepts that transcend birth and death, and leads us into the fourth and higher dimensions of consciousness where we discover the reality of the soul and encounter the energy of spirit.

We face a major stumbling block when relating the belief structures of science, religion, and psychology—finding the common ground on which to build a unifying belief system. Science deals exclusively with the physical world and the material aspect of our existence. Psychology deals exclusively with the mind and the mental aspect of our lives. Religion maintains a mysterious balancing act between the material and the spiritual world, and at the same time provides us a perspective on life that transcends death. Each of these belief systems deals with different aspects of our reality and each has its own vocabulary. In this respect, the following words written by P.D. Ouspensky in the early part of this century are as meaningful today as they were then.

> We fail to understand many things because we specialize too easily
> and too drastically, philosophy, religion, psychology, natural

sciences, sociology, etc. Each has their own special literature. There is nothing embracing the whole in its entirety.[1]

The lay person is confronted with two problems: first, the difficulty of comprehending the meaning of specialized terms; and, second, the correlation of meaning between different realms of thought. In reality, the lay person is only slightly more handicapped than the specialists, since they too, have difficulty understanding the vocabulary of other specializations. Pastors find it difficult to understand scientists and psychologists; scientists find it difficult to understand psychologists and pastors; and psychologists find it difficult to understand pastors and scientists. Our knowledge has become more and more differentiated. We have a situation where both lay persons and specialists lack the understanding necessary to bring together our belief systems into a holistic framework. Clearly, however, all the different areas of modern knowledge must have significant interrelationships. We need to identify and explore these linkages if we are to develop a belief system that unifies science, religion and psychology. The connecting principle I propose to explore is consciousness.

Science and consciousness

Up to the turn of the last century science was replete with objectivity. Scientists assumed that there was no connection between the experiment and the experimenter and that time was absolute. Two scientific theories changed these beliefs. The theory of relativity explains the movement of the macro world of planets and stars and changed our beliefs about time; and quantum theory, explains the micro world of the atom, and changed our beliefs about objectivity. These theories invited major technological innovations and verifiable explanations of our universe, made the observer a participator, and led us to recognize that time is a fluid concept intimately linked to the experience of the observer. Up to that point, physics did not recognize that the observer had any role or influence on the outcome of experiments—as if the phenomena being examined and the observer existed in two separate unconnected worlds. The first crack in this shell of objectivity came with the arrival of Einstein's Theory of Relativity. He showed that time is relative to the position and movement of an observer. Thus, time could not be considered absolute. The full impact of this discovery has not yet been absorbed into our everyday thinking. Further evidence of the important role of the observer came along in the 1930s in the form of quantum theory. To make sense of quantum experiments the observer chooses what he or she wants to measure. The outcome of such experiments is affected by the consciousness and beliefs of the observer. Fritjof Kapra, in *The Tao of Physics* describes it this way:

> Quantum theory has abolished the notion of fundamentally separated objects, it has introduced the concept of the participator to replace that of the observer, and may even find it necessary to include the human consciousness in its description of the world.[2]

Scientists have discovered that matter and energy are equivalent. All matter is a manifestation of energy. The building blocks of matter can exist as either electrically charged particles or as waves of information. The reality of the particle is three-dimensional. It has specific properties that can be measured in physical terms. The reality of the wave is four-dimensional. It is an energy field that spreads out in space and time and cannot be localized. It has no mass and no material substance. Thus, everything in our physical universe is composed of matter and at the same time is contained within an energy field that is "invisible" to our physical senses. In the wave form one finds information that describes the full potentialities of the material particle. In the physical form one finds only one of those potentialities expressed. All material objects, including our own bodies, have a three-dimensional physical form and fourth-dimensional energy field. One is in a state of being. The other is in a state of potential being.

The manifestation of a potential state of being is controlled by our thoughts . . . a belief in a potential future influences the manifestation of that future.

Paul Davies suggests that the lesson of the quantum is that matter can achieve concrete, well-defined existence only in conjunction with mind.[3] In other words, the material aspect of a "substance," exists only when there is an observing consciousness present. At all other times it remains a wave of pure potentiality. The manifestation of a potential state of being is controlled by our thoughts. In other words, a belief in a potential future influences the manifestation of that future.

If all matter is energy then the distinction between animate and inanimate matter has no meaning. When energy takes on a form, consciousness is present. It is consciousness that molds energy into matter. David Bohm, one of the world's most respected quantum physicists, put it this way.

> The ability of form to be active is the most characteristic feature of mind, and we have something that is mind like already with the electron. Even a rock is in some way alive, for life and intelligence are present in all of matter.[4]

This physicist's description of matter correlates closely with esoteric teachings. According to esoteric principles, consciousness is present in all matter. It permeates all things—atoms, molecules, plants, animals, and the earth. We live in a totally sentient world molded by the energy of thought. In *Bridging Science and Spirit*, Norman Friedman concludes, "reality is not composed of separate elements . . . reality at its most fundamental level is consciousness."[5]

Religion and consciousness

Religious experiences are described by those who have experienced them as heightened awareness and a change in consciousness. The experience takes place in the mind through the raising of awareness to a higher state of consciousness. We talk to God through prayer and we listen to God during moments of quiet contemplation. The definition William James gave to religion at the turn of the century, we would probably give to spirituality today.

The feelings, acts and experiences of individuals in their solitude, so far as they apprehend themselves to stand in relation to whatever they may consider the divine.[6]

The relationship between an individual and what he or she considers divine exists entirely in the realm of consciousness. What is important to the relationship is its content. And the content is expressed through knowledge, founded in belief, and supported by faith. Without inner experiences and the transfer of knowledge, religion becomes an empty vessel.

There are three essential points we should note about religious experiences. First, they take place in the mind. Second, they are accompanied by an increase in knowledge and a change in consciousness. And third, they are often, but not always, related to experiences of suffering and death. The hallmarks of religious experiences comprise ineffability and expansion of knowledge. Words inadequately describe the experience. At the same time, a revelation through insight, although inexpressible, leaves a profound impression.

Buddhist monasteries, Hindu temples and Christian churches methodically cultivate this type of consciousness. The elevation of consciousness based on meditation, detaches the mind from outer sensations. Saint John of the Cross describes this process as "dark contemplation." Saint Teresa describes it the following way.

The soul is fully awake as regards God, but wholly asleep as regards things of this world and in respect of herself. During the short time the union lasts, she is as it was deprived of every feeling even if she would, she could not think of any single thing . . . In short, she is utterly dead to the things of the world.[7]

Although higher states of consciousness can yield insights into the past and the future, the most important revelations flowing from higher states of consciousness are theological or metaphysical.

> Saint Ignatious confessed one day . . . that a single hour of meditation had taught him more truths about heavenly things than all the teachings of all doctors put together could have taught him.[8]

Religious experience is fundamentally an experience of a higher dimension of consciousness. An intensely personal experience, its occurrence is more often associated with inner personal growth than with the practice or pursuit of orthodox religion. Religious institutions and churches can have a major impact on our beliefs and on our reality. They can be a power for good, providing a framework within which humans can join together in common worship of their God. However, individuals who are content to follow the conventional religious observances of their country, or race, can sometimes find themselves in a spiritually moribund environment. William James says of them:

> His religion has been made for him by others, communicated to him by tradition, determined to fixed forms by imitation and retained by habit.[9]

Religious experiences for such human beings are few and vaguely felt. The emptiness of modern religion and its effect on man is described by Carl Jung in the following way.

> ...modern man expects something from the psyche (soul) which the outer world has not given him; doubtless something which our religion ought to contain, but no longer does contain, at least for modern man. For him the various forms of religion no longer appear to come from within, from the psyche; they seem more like items from the inventory of the outside world. No spirit not of this world vouchsafes him inner revelation; instead he tries on a variety of religions and beliefs as if they were Sunday attire, only to lay them aside again like worn-out clothes.[10]

Man is searching for inner knowledge. After centuries of blind faith, we are witnessing the flowering of a personal search for the truth about the inner self. This has led to a greater interest in astrology, psychology, psychic phenomena, parapsychology, spiritualism, and theosophy, among others. The fundamental characteristic of this movement is a search for knowledge through experience. Jung states:

> Modern man abhors faith and the religions based upon it. He holds them valid only so far as their knowledge—content seems to accord with his own experience of the psychic background. He wants to know—to experience for himself.[11]

This radical change in awareness is due to the success of science in explaining our three-dimensional world. When the Christian Church lost its hold over our beliefs, mankind embraced the concept of knowledge rather than faith. The new religions increasingly emphasize direct experience and often contain a veneer of science. For many people, dogma, ritualized worship, and objectification of God denuded Christianity of mystical experience. Because of this, there are a growing number of people pursuing the path of spirituality. The quest for religious experience takes place within the minds of these men and women as they search for meaning in the higher realms of consciousness.

Psychology and consciousness

Consciousness forms an integral part of psychology through theories that attempt to explain the operation of the mind. Most theories of consciousness recognize the existence of different levels of consciousness, including the subconscious and the unconscious. The understanding of the unconscious goes back to early history. Plotinus in the 2nd century, A.D., Saint Augustine in the 4th century, and Cudworth in the 17th century, refer to the limitless knowledge and intuitive characteristics of the mind.[12] The unconscious was seen as a source of wisdom and enlightenment, and as such was recognized as a true linkage with the spiritual dimensions.

The general concept of unconscious mental processes was conceived about 1700, and became fashionable between 1870-1880. Gradually, the rationality of science took over and by the beginning of the 19th century a form of psychiatry, divorced from religion, began to take form. By the end of the century, the study of the psyche had lost its religious overtones and was regarded as a scientific phenomenon. The first pole of consciousness to be understood was the ego. The ego was defined as the personality component of the self that is conscious, most immediately controls behavior, and is most in touch with external reality.

Before psychology could develop its "spiritual perspective" it first had to complete its scientific development. This was mainly achieved by Freud who was, above all, a doctor and a scientist. He was the first psychiatrist to study unconscious material systematically and scientifically. Freud's principal approach was to bring to the fore unconscious material from childhood. Freud created a model of the mind divided into conscious, preconscious, and unconscious systems. The conscious system contains those ideas of which we are aware. The preconscious system contains ideas which we are not immediately aware of, but which can be brought into consciousness by focusing our awareness on them. In contrast, the unconscious system contains ideas which we repress. Carl Jung expanded Freud's theory by subdividing the unconscious into a personal and a collective unconscious. The majority of contemporary psychotherapy focuses on the personal unconscious.

In the last 30 years a series of developments, known collectively as Transpersonal Psychology, have reconnected the traumas of the mind with spiritual emergencies.[13] This new wave of theory, taking psychology into the realm of the soul and spirituality, admits the reality of the soul by incorporating, extending, and enlarging upon previous theories. Thus, the soul is being accepted as a living force within each one of us; its eternal nature is being recognized and the soul's relationship to the ego is being defined.

Regression to past events is a well-documented tool that has been used by therapists to create a cathartic response in patients. Past-life regression is similar. Instead of being limited to the present lifetime, it brings into consciousness material from previous lives. This form of regression is practiced by hundreds of therapists with amazing results. The origins of all types of phobias can be reached, understood, and erased from the present life. The belief in past lives is centuries old and more than two-thirds of the world's population espouse such ideas within the framework of eastern religious philosophies. Since these memories transcend time and space, they must be associated with the soul-mind.

One aspect of transpersonal psychotherapy which has considerable bearing on our inquiry is Multiple Personality Disorder (MPD). Researchers are finding that persons who suffer from MPD often have no knowledge of the different personalities that exist simultaneously within them. Alternative personalities may be quite dissimilar in speech, thought patterns, mood, and temperament. The different personalities have mastered different physical abilities and interpersonal skills, and may be able to speak different foreign languages. They may also suffer from different ailments. One personality may exhibit symptoms of diabetes while other personalities will not. One personality may exhibit nearsightedness and another may be farsighted; one may be right-handed and another left-handed.

A Chicago-based psychiatrist, Bennett Braun, reported a case of a woman who exhibited burn marks on her skin when a certain alter personality emerged in therapy.[14] The burn marks would disappear when a different personality was present. This woman had been severely tortured in childhood by her brother and mother who had extinguished cigarettes on her arm. Scott Miller, a California-based psychologist, reports a case of a patient in the throes of heroin withdrawal who became symptom-free once another personality took control.[15]

During therapy it is normal for the therapist to discover one personality that is always the inner self-helper. This personality is always cooperative, shows great insight, has no negative emotions, and is cheerful and compassionate. This personality appears in all cases of MPD. Unlike other alternates whose origin can be traced back through hypnosis to a particular traumatic period the inner self-helper is likely to say, "I have always been."[16]

Several conclusions can be drawn from this brief overview of the relation of science, religion and psychology to consciousness. First, consciousness is present in all matter. Second, matter is molded by consciousness through the energy associated with our thoughts and beliefs. Third, as we shift our awareness to higher states of consciousness, we move into a realm of joy and peace. Everything exists in these higher states of consciousness as a field of energy. At

If we are to fully understand our three-dimensional reality, we need to explore the energy field of the fourth dimension of consciousness.

any one moment in time, the energy field expresses itself in a specific physical form, but it has the potential to express itself in other forms at other times according to our thoughts and beliefs. If we are to fully understand our three-dimensional reality, we need to explore the energy field of the fourth dimension of consciousness. The energy field contains all the information on our past history and on our potential for the future. It is the seat of the soul.[16]

Quantum physics has amply confirmed that matter may be understood as very dense energy. The body may be perceived and understood as energy rather than matter. D.J. Benoir and R. Benoir

Matter is the vehicle for the manifestation of soul on this plane of existence, and soul is the vehicle on a higher plane for the existence of spirit, and these are a trinity synthesized by life, which pervades them all. Helena Blavatsky

With ordinary consciousness you can't even begin to know what's happening. Saul Bellow

It is one of the commonest of mistakes to consider that the limit of our power of perception is also the limit of all there is to perceive. C.W. Leadbeater

The distinction between past, present and future is only an illusion, albeit a stubborn one. Albert Einstein

3

The Fourth Dimension of Consciousness

The root of our difficulty in understanding the fourth dimension of consciousness is our perception. We perceive the world and interact with it through five physical senses. Everything we personally know about the external world is experienced through a combination of these senses. Our senses are limited and consequently at odds with much of what science tells us. For example, we can stand in a field surrounded by trees on a beautiful calm day and nothing will move. All is still and quiet. In reality we are standing on the surface of a globe spinning on its axis and turning in space around a sun millions of miles away. We are unable to sense any of this motion and yet if a slight breeze was to arise we would sense it immediately. Similarly, we can be standing on a street corner in New York, on Sunday, and on Tuesday we can be standing on a street corner in Sydney, Australia. On one of these street corners we are upside down compared to the other, but we do not sense it. There are vast ranges of sound that we cannot hear and there are vast ranges of radiation we cannot see or feel. Science tells us that when you break down matter into its component parts everything is reduced to energy. Unless we awaken our inner senses we cannot see or feel that energy. All we see is the physical form that it takes, as if we are trapped within a body that only allows us to experience a very small part of reality—the third dimension of consciousness.

Science has long understood that we live in a multi-dimensional universe. Einstein, who was familiar with this concept, once said:

> The non mathematician is seized by a mysterious shuddering when he hears of four dimensional things, by a feeling that is not unlike the occult. But there is no more commonplace statement than the world in which we live is a four dimensional continuum.[1]

We live in a multi-dimensional world, but because of the limitations of our senses and beliefs, our awareness is focused in three-dimensional consciousness. Three-dimensionality is not a property of the world but a property of our senses.

The reality of the fourth dimension seems difficult for us to experience and comprehend. A world where space and time become interwoven in a single continuum challenges our senses and our beliefs. Even though Einstein showed us that energy and mass are interchangeable ($E=mc^2$), a world that is totally based on energy is almost impossible for us to conceive.

Three-dimensionality is not a property of the world but a property of our senses.

One way we can begin to understand the fourth dimension of consciousness is by comparing the awareness that exists in a two-dimensional world with the awareness that exists in a three-dimensional world. By extrapolating the results we can get a sense of how four-dimensional consciousness compares to three-dimensional consciousness. The way we do this is by performing what I call the five-finger exercise.

Five-finger exercise
Take a sheet of paper and lay it down on a flat surface. Imagine that there is a very small person living on the surface of this paper. This person lives in "Flatland." For this person, the world has length and breadth, but no height. In other words, this person lives in two-dimensional consciousness. Along comes a human being in three-

dimensional consciousness and places the fingers of one hand on the surface of Flatland.

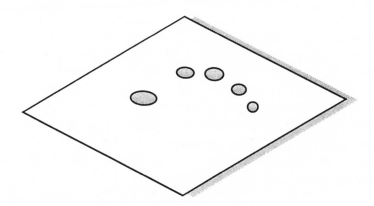

Figure 2: The projection of five fingers into
two-dimensional consciousness

Imagine that the person living in Flatland is out for a morning stroll. When passing this place yesterday, he noticed nothing unusual. Suddenly, overnight, five separate circles have appeared (the projection into two-dimensional consciousness of the five fingers). The two-dimensional being is mystified by the appearance of the five circles. He calls a friend, a two-dimensional scientist, and asks her to explain the nature of the five circles. The scientist explores the five circles using her two-dimensional logic. Her experiments show that the circles can move independently within certain limits, but if she puts a force on one circle, eventually it will appear to drag the remainder of the circles with it (although the fingers of the hand appear to be separate, they are connected in a dimension of consciousness that the two-dimensional beings cannot perceive). The two-dimensional scientist repeats her experiments. She builds equations to verify the relationship of the circles to each other and before long she believes that she knows everything there is to know about the five circles. She calls a meeting of the academy of two-dimensional scientists to show them her discovery. The two-dimensional scientists repeat the experiments and get similar results. Everyone in the two-dimensional world believes they know all there is to know about the five circles.

Viewed from the perspective of three-dimensional consciousness we know that these are not five separate circles. They are five fingers of a hand that belong to a living organism. The two-dimensional beings were unaware of this larger reality. They believed the five circles to be physically separate, but recognized that they were somehow linked, probably through a type of force field. They had an incomplete sense of the connectedness of the fingers because they could not perceive the higher dimension of consciousness.

This is the situation we find ourselves in with regard to the fourth dimension. We have countless experiences that appear unconnected, but in reality are linked, and have their cause in the fourth or higher dimensions of consciousness. Some we try to explain with our three-dimensional logic—the domain of science—and some are simply inexplicable. These we classify as paranormal, synchronistic, or mystical experiences. We use these convenient classification systems to cover our ignorance.

When we concentrate our awareness exclusively on the third dimension, we focus on a world of symbols and effects, the cause of which can lie in the third, fourth, or higher dimensions of consciousness. The average person relying on three-dimensional senses simply is unaware of the connectivity and unity that exists in the higher dimensions of consciousness.

There is one more point we should consider about the five-finger exercise. Just as the two-dimensional beings experiencing the phenomena of "fingers" did not suspect that the fingers were operated by the mind of a three-dimensional being, so we in our three-dimensional world are unaware of the control that our souls exercise in our lives. Certain events manifest in our lives because our soul has chosen them as learning experiences for our personality. There is no chance. Nor is everything predestined. The soul is able to set up potential learning experiences for us because it operates at a level of consciousness in which it is in touch with other souls.

When we come together with other people in meaningful situations it is, in effect, a collaboration of souls; but to most of us, living in three-dimensional consciousness, it appears to be a chance event.

Let us use another analogy. Take a comb and cover up the top half. What you see are the unconnected teeth of the comb. When you uncover the top half you can see that the teeth are joined together at a higher level. Indeed, the comb without the higher level connection would fall apart and could not fulfill its purpose.

As human beings, this is how we are. We perceive ourselves in three-dimensional consciousness as separate human beings like the teeth of the comb. When we raise our awareness to a higher plane of consciousness, we can see the connection. Just as the separate teeth have no meaning until we are aware that they belong to a comb, so, too, it is difficult to comprehend our own self and purpose until we become aware of our soul.

We do not have a clear understanding about what is really going on in our physical world. The logic we use to explain events is purely three-dimensional. Just as the two-dimensional scientist believed she knew all there was to know about the five circles, so do we believe that we know everything there is to know about three-dimensional phenomena. Science, and particularly medicine, are caught up in explaining three-dimensional events that often have their roots in the mind and the higher realms of consciousness.

Since science offers verifiable and measurable results, we tend to believe that everything exists within the limits of our three-dimensional awareness while, in fact, much of what we are striving to comprehend is rooted in other levels of consciousness of which we are only dimly aware. When you understand this, you begin to realize that our interpretation of events is mostly fragmentary and a product of intense rationalization from an incomplete base of knowledge. We are like the two-dimensional scientist, trying to explain something that cannot be fully explained unless we take a higher-dimensional perspective. In our normal state of awareness, we only perceive the three-dimensional perspective of our multi-dimensional world. What we see is the projection of the higher dimensions of consciousness into our three-dimensional world and we mistake it for the whole experience. In other words, we have an incomplete sense of causality.

You may ask, "Why are we not more aware of the fourth and higher dimensions of consciousness in our everyday living?" The answer is that we have blocked out this perspective of our reality through three-dimensional conditioning. As children, many of us were in touch with this reality. We were told that the beings of energy that we saw and communicated with simply did not exist. Gradually, we learned to deny this aspect of our reality. We closed ourselves down to the fourth dimension of consciousness. However, this ability to be in touch with other dimensions of consciousness—through intuition, telepathy, seeing auras, automatic writing, or channeling voices of nonphysical beings[2]—can be recovered. Many hundreds of thousands of people around the world are discovering that they have these abilities.

Comparing third and fourth dimensions of consciousness

To consolidate our understanding of our multidimensional reality, it is perhaps useful at this point to compare what we know about the third and fourth dimensions of consciousness. The fundamental aspects of our awareness in three-dimensional consciousness are time, space, and matter. Time and space give us the illusion of separation, time and matter give us the illusion of death and decay, and space and matter give us the illusion of mass.

The fundamental aspects of awareness in the fourth dimension of consciousness are timelessness (eternity), spacelessness (omnipresence) and energy. Without time and space to give us the illusion of separation, we experience unity. Without time and matter to give us the illusion of death and decay, we experience a permanent sense of being. Finally, without matter and space to give us the illusion of mass, we experience a constant flow of energy. In the fourth dimension of consciousness there is only an eternal moment that we call now and everything exists in energy forms.

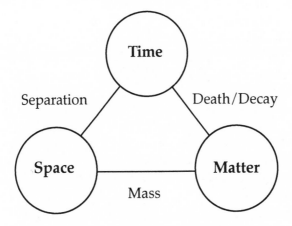

Three-dimensional awareness

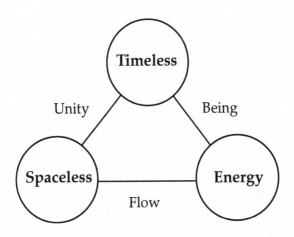

Four-dimensional awareness

Figure 3: Aspects of awareness in three- and
four-dimensional consciousness

The energy field

The aura, or energy field of the body is well known in China and India and forms the basis of their traditional healing systems. Associated with the human aura are seven major energy centers known as chakras. These are the major connecting points between the energy field and the physical body. Energy flows through the chakras and enlivens the body. The energy flows from the chakras along a fine network of channels known as the etheric body. These are the meridians used in acupuncture. When energy blocks occur in any part of the network, sickness and diseases follow. The cause of all sickness and disease begins in the energy field and manifests in the physical body.

It is important to realize that it is not the body that has an energy field, but the energy field that has a physical body. The energy field belongs to the soul. According to Barbara Brennan,there are several interconnecting energy fields contained within the cocoon of the aura.[3] The outer energy fields form the spiritual body and vibrate at a very high frequency. Contained within the spiritual body, and most closely associated with the physical world, are the mental body, the emotional body, and the etheric body. Each body vibrates at a lower frequency than the body which contains it. The physical body vibrates at the lowest frequency and is molded by the etheric body.

> *It is not the body that has an energy field, but the energy field that has a physical body.*

As the pure energy emanating from the spiritual body flows through the other bodies, the frequency of vibration slows down and the energy becomes more fragmented. The belief structures of the mental body filter and modify the energy into a unique energy pattern that is your personality. The presence of fear beliefs affect your personality's frequency of vibration. Fear causes the energy field to slow its vibrations. These modifications to the energy field that occur in the mental body are felt in the lower bodies. The heaviness you feel after a very stressful day is due to the impact your fear beliefs have on your energy system. On such a day you come home feeling worn out because your energy field has lowered its vibrational frequency. Similarly, when you have an uplifting experience, you feel your energy rise. Meditation also refreshes the body. It raises your awareness to the spiritual levels of the aura where you experience the higher frequencies of vibration, and release the lower vibrational energy of fear, replacing it with the higher vibrational energy of love.

Valerie Hunt, a physical therapist and professor of kinesiology with the University of California at Los Angeles, has developed a way to confirm experimentally the existence of the human energy field and has measured the range of frequencies it can operate under.[4] Science has long been aware of electromagnetic fields in the body. Hunt was able to measure the electrical activity of the human energy field outside the body. She found that most people whose consciousness is firmly focused in the physical world had energy fields in a range of frequencies around 250 cycles per second, close to the body's own biological frequencies. Hunt found that people with psychic or healing abilities had frequencies of 400 to 800 cycles per second in their energy field. Trance channelers skip these frequencies and operate in a narrow band between 800 and 900 cycles per second. Frequencies above 900 cycles per second correspond to mystical personalities. Hunt has encountered people with frequencies as high as 200,000 cycles per second. These higher vibrational personalities appear to be in touch with other levels of consciousness. They are aware of the cosmic interrelatedness of all things. For these people the world is experienced as a unified energy field.

Seven levels of consciousness

According to various philosophical and religious traditions, our multidimensional minds have the ability to experience seven levels of consciousness. The first three—waking, dreaming and deep sleep —are part of everyone's daily experiences. In the fourth level of consciousness you transcend the sense of the physical, and experience your soul. This state of consciousness can be attained through meditation. During periods of meditation (also known as the relaxation response) the body and its neurological systems experience pure relaxation. At the same time, the mind basks in a realm of peace, joy, and love beyond space and time and three-dimensional belief systems. Study after study shows that frequent meditators live longer, have less hospital and doctors' visits, and maintain a more positive outlook than non-meditators.

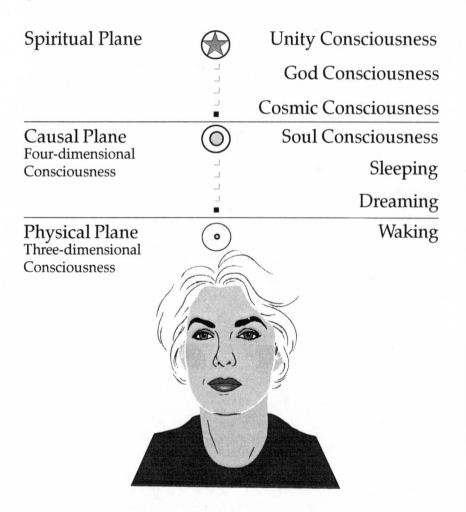

Spiritual Plane		Unity Consciousness
		God Consciousness
		Cosmic Consciousness
Causal Plane Four-dimensional Consciousness		Soul Consciousness
		Sleeping
		Dreaming
Physical Plane Three-dimensional Consciousness		Waking

Figure 4: The seven levels of consciousness

Meditation is particularly beneficial for improving interpersonal relations, and is particularly beneficial for those suffering from heart disease. The more frequent the periods of meditation, the more lasting the effects.

Beyond the fourth level of consciousness, or soul consciousness, lies a fifth state, known as cosmic consciousness. In this state of soul consciousness your personality and soul become permanently indistinguishable. Your personality remains totally identified with the your soul at all times and you experience a fear-free state of mental and physiological functioning. In this state, group consciousness supports all impulses of thought and feeling, and you effortlessly fulfill you desires while simultaneously supporting the interests of others. In this state you operate fully on the principle of self-referral. That is to say, you are able to live your life to its fullness without ever feeling the need to seek approval from any individual or institution. This gives you freedom to become fully self-actualized.

At the sixth level of consciousness, known as God consciousness, you are able to fully experience the oneness with all the various manifestations of soul. You are completely aware of the soul aspect of all other forms of life. There remains but the finest sense of separation between your awareness and the awareness of all other souls. In this state of consciousness an intimate connection is developed between self and everything else. Physical creation is glorified. Finally, at the seventh level you achieve unity consciousness. At this level you experience the highest value of self-referral. The self fuses with the self aspect of every other form of creation in total oneness. There is no separation between the knower and the object of knowing. This represents the culmination of soul development.

The soul manifests in three-dimensional consciousness to learn lessons that will allow it to evolve toward unity consciousness. The personality can help or hinder the soul. By seeking to align your personality with your soul you can assist your soul to fulfill its purpose. To cooperate fully, you must shift your perspective from the third to the fourth dimension of consciousness. You must learn to understand life from the point of view of your soul.

Mind is consciousness that has put on limitations.
Ramana Maharshi

The overall number of minds is just one. Edwin Schrodinger

When we align our thoughts, emotions and actions with the highest part of ourselves, we are filled with enthusiasm, purpose and meaning. Gary Zukav

We do not see things as they are, but as we are. The Talmud

In the final analysis we must love in order not to fall ill.
Sigmund Freud

When we are unable to find tranquility within ourselves, it is useless to seek it elsewhere. La Rochefoucauld

4
Who Am I?

Throughout history there is one phrase above all others that has been recognized as holding the key to wisdom—"Know thyself." This phrase was etched in stone above the entrance to the temple of Apollo in Delphi, and is referred to as the "highest light" in the Hindu holy texts, *The Upanishads*. Achieving an understanding of oneself is a difficult task, but also one of the most rewarding. Many attempt to reach such an understanding by leading a life of contemplation and study, or spending time in retreats. The insights reached can be rewarding, but they do not take on meaning until you try to implement them in your daily life. That is the difficult part. Although it is relatively easy to experience peace and harmony in the privacy of your room, or by living in a spiritual community, when you leave your sanctuary and move into the larger world, your inner peace shatters in an instant if you have not fully integrated the insights of self-knowledge into your life. Only through internalizing the vicissitudes of life do you truly come to know yourself.

One mind
The search for self-knowledge takes us on a journey into consciousness and leads us directly into the mind, for it is there that we find the true expression of our being. The body is simply the vehicle of the mind in three-dimensional consciousness. Before going further, let us define a few basic terms that we will encounter frequently in

the remainder of this book—brain, mind, consciousness, soul, and spirit. The brain is a physical organ contained within space and time and that part of the central nervous system enclosed in the cranium that controls and coordinates the autonomic and immune systems.

Contrary to popular opinion, the brain is *not* the storehouse of our memories. If the brain physically stored memories then we should be able to find particular memories associated with specific parts of the brain. Karl Lashley's

> *Only through internalizing the vicissitudes of life do you truly come to know yourself.*

research confirms that this is not the case. He trained rats to perform a variety of tasks and then surgically removed various portions of their brains. He found that no matter what portion of the brain he removed, the rats could still repeat the tasks they had learned. He concluded that memories are not located in any specific brain sites.[1] This suggests that the mind, not the brain, is the storehouse for our memories.

The mind differs from the brain. Since it is not a physical organ the mind cannot be located in space and time and cannot be perceived by our senses. The mind's principal attribute is consciousness. It is the crucible of our thoughts and our connection to higher states of consciousness.

When the body dies, the organizing force that gives life to the body and makes it a functioning whole returns completely to the fourth-dimension of consciousness. The physical body then starts to decay. That organizing force is the soul. The energy that gives life to the body and the soul is called spirit. Soul molds the body; spirit energizes the body. When the soul retires from the body, the spirit energy belonging to the soul retires with it. Without the life force and organizing principle of the soul, there is nothing to hold together the cells of the body. They lose their cohesiveness, disintegrate, and return to basic chemical elements. When we bury our dead, we return these elements to the ground from where they came.

Those that believe in any form of life after death usually regard the soul as the "entity" that transcends death. If the mind continues to exhibit awareness after death then it must be contained within the soul. Verbal accounts from those who were declared clinically dead and came back to life (near-death experiences, or NDEs) clearly suggest that awareness continues outside the body. Thus, soul and mind must be regarded as part of the same entity. Reviewing the stories of those who have had near death experiences, Michael Talbot concludes that persons experiencing NDEs see and know things that they have no normal sensory means of seeing and knowing.[2] Those who have been declared clinically dead, with no brain activity even for several hours, and have come back to life, appear not to have noticed a change in awareness even though they were absent from their body. In many cases they actually saw their body lying beneath them. Could these memories be recorded in a brain that had ceased activity? Or, are they part of the mind? Talbot concludes that NDEs offer ample evidence that the mind exists independently of the brain.

The mind not only allows us to be in touch with other dimensions of consciousness, but it also allows us to transcend space and time.

Those who have experienced an NDE are almost always transformed. They become happier, more optimistic and easygoing, and less concerned about material possessions. Most strikingly of all, their capacity to love expands enormously and parallels an increased interest in spirituality.[3] The experience occurs in the fourth dimension of consciousness. They have been in touch with their soul.

Consciousness occurs when you have an awareness of your own existence and environment. Science tells us that the human species is the only species that is aware that it is aware. Creatures and plants exhibit consciousness, but are less aware of their own individuality. They tend to operate in group consciousness. The lowest form of creatures may have no group or individual awareness. They may simply be aware of their environment. In higher states of consciousness humans connect with other souls while maintaining their individuality.

The mind not only allows us to be in touch with other dimensions of consciousness, but it also allows us to transcend space and time. Telepathy, the ability to communicate information between minds without the aid of the physical senses, is a well-known phenomenon. Telepathic messages are not affected by spatial separation. A person with telepathic abilities can just as easily receive and send information over long distances as short distances. However, senders are not even necessary. To be aware of events in other times and places, without being there is entirely possible.

A well-authenticated example concerns Emanuel Swedenborg, a Swedish scientist, religious teacher, and mystic. While staying in Gothenberg, away from his hometown of Stockholm, he had a vision at about six o'clock in the evening of a fire in the district near his home. He saw the home of his friend already reduced to ashes and his own home in danger. At eight o'clock he declared the fire stopped three houses away from his home. The precise events and their timing were confirmed a few days later.

This ability of the mind to tap into other levels of consciousness is a theme explored by Larry Dossey in his book *Recovering the Soul*.[4] Dossey, a physician, provides a wide-ranging scientific, religious, and philosophical synthesis of the evidence to support the idea that there exists within the human mind a level of consciousness shared by all mankind and every living creature. Dossey recounts, in a series of separate experiments, how student researchers were set up to believe that specific groups of students, rats, and worms were more intelligent than other groups. After a certain period of time during which the "intelligent" and "not-so-intelligent" groups received identical training, the intelligent groups seemed to test much better than the unintelligent groups. In fact, the groups were constituted at random, but the experimenters were not told this. The conclusion drawn was that the beliefs in the minds of the experimenters influenced the performance of the students, rats, and worms. The experimenters actually influenced the different groups at a shared level of consciousness. Other experiments with rats, verified by many experimenters, show that successive generations of rats descended from trained parents learn to perform experiments quicker and quicker. However, the successive generations of untrained rats in the control line *also* learned quicker and quicker. Whereas in the first experiments, described above, we discussed the communication of human beliefs to other humans and animals, this case deals with the communication of acquired knowledge between animals themselves. Dossey sums up his explanation of what he calls the "non-local mind" in the following way:

> In the end we can choose to continue to believe that we are local, isolated, doomed creatures confined to time and the body and set apart from all other human beings [and the animal and plant kingdoms]. Or we may elect to open our eyes to our immortal, omnipresent nature and the One Mind of which we each are a part. If we choose the former, nothing will save us. If, however, we choose to awaken to our divine Self, we face a new dawn.[5]

He gives us a choice. We can believe the perceptions of our senses and live a life rooted in and restricted to three-dimensional consciousness. Or, we can recognize the multidimensional nature of our mind and of its connection with all creation.

The physicist David Bohm suggests that everything in the universe is part of such a continuum. We humans, and all matter, are reducible to energy forms. In this state we are all constituted from the same "substance." Indeed, Bohm believes that our tendency to fragment the world and ignore the dynamic interconnectedness of all things is responsible for all our problems.

Our tendency to fragment the world is responsible for all our problems.

We see every problem in isolation from the larger picture, and spend our time trying to treat symptoms rather than getting to the root causes.[6] Sri Aurobindo, an Indian mystic, agrees with Bohm. He states that all separateness is an illusion. All things are ultimately connected and whole. Our level of consciousness is directly proportional to the degree of fragmentation we allow into our beliefs about whom we are.[7]

If our consciousness forms part of a soul-mind, why are we not immediately aware of our past lives? The answer is, that at the soul level of our consciousness, we *are* aware, but at the level of three-dimensional consciousness, we are not. When the soul incarnates, the conscious memories of the soul become the unconscious memories of the personality. These memories can be accessed through meditation and hypnosis by shifting your awareness to the soul dimension of consciousness.

A model of the mind

This understanding of the relationship between the soul and the personality can be found in the work of the Italian transpersonal psychiatrist Roberto Assagioli.[8, 9]

Assagioli (1888-1974), born in Venice, devoted his life to the development of the branch of psychotherapy known as psychosynthesis. The techniques of psychosynthesis gained a considerable following in therapeutic circles since the late 1950s. The basic difference between psychosynthesis and classical psychoanalysis is that the former recognizes the existence of the soul. Whereas most psychotherapists are interested only in a client's personality, in psychosynthesis the client is regarded as a soul with a personality. The treatment reintegrates , or attunes, the personality with the soul. The therapist works with the whole spectrum of consciousness and brings together (synthesis) fragmented parts of the client's repressed personality. The soul is regarded as basic and enduring, while the personality is considered superficial and changing. In psychosynthesis we find a bridge between religion and psychology. Assagioli developed a model of the mind which contains the soul.

The oval shape in Figure 5 represents all aspects of our personal psyche, including the soul dimension. In the center of the oval is pure self-awareness that derives from the soul—the projection of the soul into three-dimensional consciousness. Surrounding this soul-self, which Assagioli refers to as the "I," is a field of consciousness in which we create our three-dimensional reality. This is the domain of the ego, and comprises an incessant flow of emotions, thoughts, and images. The ego and the soul-self together make up your unique personality. You can choose where to focus your awareness, either in the ego or the soul-self. When you choose the soul-self, you have immediate access to your soul and the high vibrational love energies that surround it. When you choose the ego, you access the lower vibrational energies of fear.

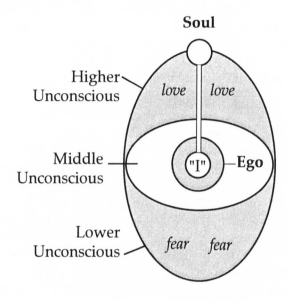

Figure 5: A model of the mind

To experience the inner world of the soul-mind, you must focus your awareness on the soul-self, the "I." This involves tuning out the thoughts generated by the ego, and moving your awareness to the center of your being. This inward movement of consciousness allows you to leave behind the concerns and worries of the ego. When your mind is quiet and focused on the soul-self, you can reach upwards to access your soul and higher levels of consciousness.

The process of relinquishing the ego and the turmoil of three-dimensional awareness is a form of cleansing, or healing of the mind. When you do not bathe, your body gets dirty, microorganisms find a home in the filth, sores appear, and you eventually get sick. When you do not cleanse your consciousness, the same thing happens. Your ego provides a home for thoughts and beliefs that prey on the mind. You worry, you get angry, and you feel depressed. You lose control and you experience a loss of freedom. You become dominated by the external world, lost in three-dimensional consciousness. When you shift your awareness to the soul-self, you move into the domain of pure consciousness where it is washed clean of beliefs. This place of true being, where you can bask in joy and truth, releases the machinations of the ego as it wallows in its fears about the external world.

With regular practice you can detach from the ego's preoccupation with three-dimensional consciousness. As you spend time with your soul, you become an observer of the reality created by your ego. You understand why you behave in certain ways and the fears that motivate that behavior. The more you identify with your soul, the more you embrace a life without fear. You move around in your personality and observe your thought processes instead of locking into automatic responses founded in your fear-based belief systems. This is the experience of true freedom. In this state the world becomes a constant source of opportunity for you to express your talents. Until you recognize you have this place where you can detach from the emotional turmoil of your ego, you will live below your potential.

Surrounding the field of consciousness of the personality (the ego and the "I") is the middle unconscious—our personal memory bank of this present lifetime and the place where we process and rationalize our day-

To experience your soul your mind must transcend the thoughts and belief structures of the ego.

to-day experiences. Here we make judgments, develop attitudes and apply reasoning based on our beliefs. By turning the spotlight of our awareness to the middle unconscious, we can relive our past experiences in the present. We can also confront the beliefs we are prepared to own. This level, our persona, contains only that which we are prepared to accept into our reality. Those thoughts, feelings, and beliefs that we are afraid to confront lie at a deeper level in the lower unconscious and form part of our shadow.

The lower unconscious hides what we don't want to deal with and is the home of all our unacknowledged fear-based beliefs. The beliefs we find at this level are our most painful beliefs. Freud focused mainly on the lower unconscious, just as most psychoanalysts do today. Abraham Maslow wrote in 1968, "it is as if Freud supplied us with the sick half of psychology and we must now fill it with the healthy half."[10] Psychosynthesis does just that: the soul is introduced into the map of the mind in the form of the higher unconscious.

The higher unconscious is the realm of your soul. At this level you are in touch with other souls, guides, teachers, and helpers. In this fourth dimension of consciousness your soul knows everything about the life you lead. Your soul knows why it incarnated, what it hopes to achieve, and why it chose particular circumstances for its life experience. To experience your soul you must transcend the thoughts and belief structures of the ego to reach that point of peace and stillness that is the "I." Very much like moving into the center of the eye ("I") of a storm, you find a place of quiet where the turmoil ceases. From the "I" you ascend through the center of the vortex to a place above the storm. As you do this, you raise your awareness to a higher level of consciousness and increase your ability to access soul knowledge through intuition.

Viewed from the perspective of the soul, the ego is unreal; its thoughts totally derive from beliefs. As long as we hang onto our beliefs, we remain firmly embedded in three-dimensional consciousness. When we quiet our mind, thought ceases, and we transcend our beliefs. We move out of our ego into our soul-self. Only then can we gain access to our soul. When we are in touch with our soul, we have a direct link to the one mind.

Attunement

Attunement, also known as spiritual unfoldment, is the process of bringing your ego into harmony with your soul. Attunement occurs when your personality and your soul merge. In this state of consciousness, you experience unconditional love. Everything is in a state of perfection. Nothing is out of place. To reach this state you must release your fears and learn to live in soul consciousness.

Three-dimensional consciousness provides you the signposts you need to proceed along the pathway of attunement. Each time you feel any form of emotional or physical discomfort, then you have allowed the fears of the ego to overcome the love of the soul. Pain and discomfort derive their being from an absence of love. The distress you feel is a measure of the lack of attunement with the soul. Ultimately, the only hope to be free of suffering is to embrace your soul and bring unconditional love into every aspect of your life. Learning to live in soul consciousness requires learning to live in realms of consciousness beyond the third dimension. It is a voyage of discovery into territory that we have forgotten we owned. All that is required is remembering who you are. The soul-self is our connection to the soul and higher dimensions of consciousness. This place of calm and quiet at the center of our awareness does not impose itself. It waits patiently for recognition, while around it the ego constructs a world of turmoil and illusions founded on fear-based beliefs.

You are given the gift of the gods; you create your own reality according to your beliefs. Yours is the creative energy that makes your world. There are no limitations to the self except those you believe in. Seth

You cannot expect the world to change until you change yourself. Robert Muller

The key to life is to understand that nothing can happen to you, nothing can ever come to you or be kept from you except in accord with your state of consciousness. Paul Twitchell

What we are today comes from our thoughts of yesterday, and our present thoughts build our lives of tomorrow. Our life is the creation of the mind. Gautama the Buddha

Only you can deprive yourself of anything. Do not oppose this realization for it is truly the beginning of the dawn of light.
A Course in Miracles

5

Why Am I Living This Reality?

The most painful moments of our lives invite us to reflect on such profound questions as, "Why am I living this reality? Why was I born to this gender, with this body, with these strengths and these weaknesses, or with this handicap?" Responses to these questions remain mysteries which science, religion, and psychology cannot answer. Three-dimensional logic breaks down when confronted with causes emanating from the fourth and higher levels of consciousness. Because of our difficulty in overcoming the limitations imposed by our three-dimensional senses, we respond to such questions with the label "chance." We invented the concept of chance to compensate for the limited scope of our three-dimensional knowledge. We use the word "chance" to cloak our ignorance. When we are focused in the physical plane of consciousness, we are completely unaware that many of our life circumstances are a direct result of the interventions of our soul. The soul intervenes in three fundamental ways.

Soul interventions

First, prior to your present incarnation your soul determined the physical situations in which you find yourself in this life (gender, race, physical form, proclivity and vulnerability to certain diseases). Previous incarnations reflect your present psychic inheritance. Who you are now is the result of an evolutionary process that your soul has been involved in for thousands of years. The situation in which you find yourself in this life was determined by your soul to facilitate a particular learning experience. Your psychic and physical disposition are functions of the state of evolution of your consciousness.

Your family and the important people in your life are incarnations of souls that lived with you in previous lifetimes. They form part of your "soul family." When a soul incarnates in human form, it does so with other members of its soul family. Your parents, siblings, spouse, and children are very often souls that are intimately familiar with your soul. When you encounter people with whom you have an immediate affinity and unnatural degree of trust, it is highly likely that you had a close relationship with this person in a previous lifetime. These are also souls that you have journeyed with before.

The forms of the intervention of the soul are always loving, although they may involve what appear to be negative or painful situations.

Because of these close ties at the soul level, a soul will sometimes incarnate not to work on its own lessons, but to contribute to the learning of others. This may be the case when a child dies at a very young age. The lesson here may be for the parents to seek a deeper understanding and meaning to life as part of their unfoldment process. This type of help from a kindred soul is a loving gesture. Our soul family is there to help us learn our lessons as we are there to help them learn their lessons. At the soul level there is no hatred or malice, everything is perfectly understood.

The second way your soul intervenes in your life is to instigate challenging situations connected to the lessons you are learning. They can take the form of a life-threatening disease, an accident, a near-death experience, or a permanent handicap. Your soul designs the event, or circumstances, to make you reflect on your life. It could be an accident, or someone bringing you a life-changing message you are ready to hear. The forms of the soul's intervention are always loving, although they may involve what appear to be negative and painful situations. The soul intervenes due to the personality's failure to tackle the lessons the soul has designed for this lifetime. The soul tries to get the attention of the personality by creating life challeng-ing circumstances. However, when these attempts fail, the soul may simply decide to pull out of its present life experience through a fatal accident, or by contracting a fatal disease.

A colleague of mine, who was a confirmed workaholic, spent the majority of his life running from one project to another. Twice as productive as anyone I knew, he worked long hours and always traveled. One day he fell and broke his hip. This put him in bed for several weeks, but he didn't stop working. He simply connected his portable computer to the hospital telephone line and continued communicating with his colleagues. Reports and letters were brought over to him regularly. He kept living his life the way he had always lived it. Oblivious to the real meaning of his accident, the slowdown message was not received. Within six months he died in a car crash. The majority saw this episode of his life as a series of unfortunate circumstances, a patch of bad luck. His death seemed meaningless. I believe his soul tried to get his attention, but failed. His personality was too set in his ways to pay attention to his soul's purpose. The soul, recognizing the futility of this incarnation becoming a positive learning experience, found a way to retire from the three-dimen-sional plane of consciousness.

The third way your soul intervenes occurs when you align with your soul purpose. When you accept yourself as a *soul having a human experience*, and follow your heart, you find your soul creates opportunities for you to accomplish your soul purpose. You feel totally supported by your soul in everything you do. Your life becomes full of meaning as you witness the powerful forces of "coincidence" that you unleashed. We will explore this topic more fully in Chapters 10 and 11.

Fourth-dimensional principles
In addition to soul interventions, our lives are influenced by the laws and principles that govern the flow of energy in the fourth dimen-sion of consciousness. The most fundamental of these laws is that *the quality of energy you send out into the world is the quality of the energy you receive in return*. The energy movement you experience coming from

the outer world is always equal in quality and opposite in direction to your own energy movement. This is similar to Newton's Third Law of Motion—to every action there is an equal and opposite reaction; equal in force and opposite in direction.

For example, someone who craves love seeks to draw energy from others to fill that need. People often react to such situations by pulling away themselves. So the person who is trying to get love is constantly encountering situations where that love is denied them. If you have ever been around someone needy in this respect, you know how draining it is to be confronted with constant demands for love, especially when your responses never seem to be enough. This persons's real issue is a deep-rooted fear that he or she is not loved. This belief filter is not selective; if you have it , it operates in every relationship you have. Despite the numerous demonstrations of love you receive, you never have enough because your belief filter constantly reminds you that you are not loved.

The quality of energy you send out into the world is the quality of the energy you receive in return.

The principle also applies in the opposite sense. A person with self-esteem and a positive outlook gives out love unconditionally. A pleasure to be with such persons, they constantly give out positive energy. The energy they put out comes back to them, because they attract people also giving out positive energy. Another form of this same principle is, "You attract whatever you fear." When you try to push away something that you fear, you often end up attracting it. Let me illustrate with an example.

An acquaintance of mine had a deep-rooted fear about being alone. He married a woman with a sister. He created a business with his wife, and she invited her sister to work with her. The two sisters got along well and were almost inseparable. They worked long hours making the business successful. Because of his attitude about sharing, he resented the time that the two sisters spent together. Often on his own in the evening while they were working, he began to nag his wife to spend more time with him and he began to hate his wife's sister for keeping his wife from him. The more he nagged the more his wife spent time with her sister. The nagging literally drove his wife away. So strongly did he hate his sister-in-law that when his wife died, he fired her sister. The company soon went bankrupt and he found himself completely alone. The sister that could have comforted him was pushed away by his hate. What he feared most, "being alone," became his reality. By trying to get his needs met, he pushed away both his wife and his sister-in-law.

This principle applies to every aspect of our lives. To get whatever you believe you lack involves a sacrifice of something you do not want to lose. For example, those seeking power, money, or status, often find that they sacrifice their family life and relationships. Power, money, and status are also forms of energy. As you try to fill the void you feel inside by pulling these toward you, they tend to escape you. To get them you sacrifice your integrity and principles. In the end you find only pain and sorrow. The emptiness goes away only when you realize that as *a soul having a human experience* you have no real needs. Everything necessary is provided when you live in soul consciousness.

Understanding this principle is fundamental if you want to improve your life. The principle works on the basis of your intention. If , by giving, your real intention is to get what you feel you lack, what you want to get escapes you. Only when the giving is unconditional do you receive in return. Giving un-conditional love is the surest

Every event is neutral. You give the situations in your life all the meaning they have for you.

way to feel loved. Giving your money unconditionally to others, or for good causes, is the surest way to get a return on your capital. If your intention is to get something that you feel you lack, you always repel what you want. Conversely, whatever you give out uncondi-tionally is what you attract. When you fully understand that what you crave you push away, and what you freely give away you attract, you then have a strong incentive to begin to release the fears at the root of your cravings.

The second most important principle that involves the fourth dimension of consciousness is that *you give the events in your life all the meaning they have for you.* The emotional content of any experience is based on the set of beliefs that you have about that experience. We mistakenly believe that our emotions are reality. In fact, our emotions are only our interpretations of reality. You and I can both experience exactly the same events, but the manner in which we react to those events may be very different. This difference is simply a function of the beliefs that we have about the situation.

For example, in some societies, death is considered as a release, and funerals are a time for joy and celebration for the deceased returning to the world from which she or he came. In other societies, death is a reminder of our mortality and funerals are sad and somber occasions. Thus, the same event impacts people differently depending on their beliefs.

The rule we need to learn in its simplest form is that all events are neutral. You "choose" how to interpret the events based on your beliefs about the situation. However, sometimes you may not feel you have exercised a choice because the beliefs you hold may be hidden in your unconscious. Your reactions are always based on your beliefs about that situation. Your emotions, thoughts, and behavior reflect your beliefs.

For the scientifically inclined, one can explain this situation in the following way. When you regard an event as neutral, you identify with the "wave form." When you give the situation a particular meaning, you identify with the physical form. In the wave form every situation is full of potentialities. When consciousness intervenes, one aspect of that potential manifests into being. The aspect that manifests is the one most closely aligned with your beliefs. Eugene Wigner, a quantum scientist, explains the problem of collapsing quantum information into an actual measurement by reference to the mind. Wigner has suggested that definite outcomes are produced by the consciousness of the observer acting on the quantum system. In the fourth dimension everything exists as a wave of pure potentiality. The mind acts at this level to collapse the wave into a well-defined three-dimensional state.

You are never a victim

We can conclude from the preceding that as souls, or as personalities, we are always responsible for creating our realities. We are never the victims of circumstance. The popularly held belief that causes lie outside ourselves in the external world is just a belief. The consciousness model shows that the cause lies within us. Your mind is a projector and your life the screen. What you see on the screen of life is a perfect reflection of your inner consciousness. Accepting responsibility for your life means recognizing that, at some level, you create your own reality.

We all have a choice to make in life. We can either be responsible, or we can be victims. The first choice gives *you* the power to change your life, while the second puts you at the mercy of others. It is essential to remember that the meaning you give to events in your life is the meaning you *choose* to give them. Everything is up to you and how you see the world. You are never a victim unless you choose to be.

Your mind is a projector and your life is the screen.

Scientists are beginning to learn what philosophers have known for centuries—that mind can influence matter. However, they still have to discover the fact that mind creates and forms matter. In *The Holographic Universe,* Michael Talbot provides many examples of the impact of the mind's manipulations on the physical world, the most striking of which is the story of a man called Wright. His story comes from the case report of psychologist Bruno Klopfer. Klopfer was treating Wright who was suffering from an advanced state of cancer. Wright did not want to die and had heard about an exciting new drug called Krebiozen.

> He begged his doctor to let him try it. At first his doctor refused because the drug was only being tried on people with a life expectancy of at least three months. But Wright was so unrelenting in his entreaties, his doctor finally gave in. He gave Wright an injection of Krebiozen on Friday, but in his heart of hearts he did not expect Wright to last the weekend. Then the doctor went home.

To his surprise, on the following Monday he found Wright out of bed and walking around. Klopfer reported that his tumors had "melted like snowballs on a hot stove" and were half their original sizes. This was a far more rapid decrease in size than even the strongest radiation treatments could have accomplished. Ten days after Wright's first Krebiozen treatment, he left the hospital and was, as far as his doctors could tell, cancer free. When he had entered the hospital, he had needed an oxygen mask to breathe, but when he left he was well enough to fly his own plane at 12,000 feet with no discomfort.

Wright remained well for about two months, but then articles began to appear asserting that Krebiozen actually had no effect on cancer of the lymph nodes. Wright, who was rigidly logical and scientific in his thinking, became very depressed, suffered a relapse, and was readmitted to the hospital. This time his physician decided to try an experiment. He told Wright that Krebiozen was every bit as effective as it had seemed, but that some of the initial supplies of the drug had deteriorated during shipping. He explained, however, that he had a new highly concentrated version of the drug and could treat Wright with this. Of course the physician did not have a new version of the drug and intended to inject Wright with plain water. To create the proper atmosphere he even went through an elaborate procedure before injecting Wright with the placebo.

Again the results were dramatic. Tumor masses melted, chest fluid vanished, and Wright was quickly back on his feet and feeling great. He remained symptom-free for another two months, but then the American Medical Association announced that a nationwide study of Krebiozen had found the drug worthless in the treatment of cancer. This time Wright's faith was completely shattered. His cancer blossomed anew and he died two days later.[1]

Wright's story is tragic, but it is also illuminating. The amazing power of the mind causes physical changes in our three-dimensional reality. In other words, the mind-soul complex encompasses the ability to manipulate matter.

Of all the beautiful truths pertaining to the soul which have been restored and brought life in this age, none is more gladdening or fruitful of divine promise and confidence than this—that you are the master of your thought, the molder of your character, and the maker and shaper of your condition, environment and destiny. James Allen

You are given the gift of the gods; you create your own reality according to your beliefs. Yours is the creative energy that makes your world. There are no limitations to the self except those you believe in. Seth

We see through a glass darkly, as it is said in the Bible. The glass is our set of beliefs, our personal prejudices, our culture, the prevailing scientific theories. And the image of reality we form is a self-fulfilling prophecy. Individually and collectively, we create our reality after our own image of it. Anna Lemkow

6

The Origins of Beliefs

Beliefs originate from three sources. We acquire them from the culture and society into which we are born; we learn them from our interactions with parents and those with whom we have close relationships; and we bring them into this life as part of our soul's heritage.

Very few of our beliefs are based on hard facts. They mostly reflect our conditioning through life experiences, the mores of our culture and society, and our relationships with parents, teachers, and peers. All the models we use to explain life—science, religion, and psychology—comprise belief systems based on theories that have achieved common acceptance.

Even our economic system is based on beliefs. Investors govern the rise and fall of the stock market by what they believe is happening, or going to happen. Our collective belief agreement to operate a monetary system assigns value to pieces of metal and paper we call money. They are, in some sense, neutral tokens of a collective belief system. We give these tokens all the value they have for us through our beliefs. Someone never exposed to a monetary economy would say that the coins and bank notes we use are simply scraps of metal and bits of wood pulp made into paper. No matter where we turn, we find systems of thought based on belief. Our entire world operates on the basis of individual and collective belief systems. Without beliefs nothing would have meaning.

Acquired beliefs

Acquired beliefs are, to a very large extent, determined by the cultural and economic environment into which we are born. Although born a male into a poor Protestant family in Yorkshire, I might just as well have been born a female into the family of an Alaskan Eskimo, a rich Hindu in Bombay, or an impoverished bush tribesman in the Kalahari desert. In each case, my belief structure about the world would be significantly different. As a Yorkshire man my belief system reflects a British Protestant outlook very similar to those of my friends and relatives also living in Yorkshire.

Meanwhile, my Alaskan and Kalahari counterparts live in a very different world with different belief structures. Essential for them to live in harmony with their physical environments if they are to survive, for me physical survival is hardly even an issue. My reality is one of economic survival.

My Hindu counterpart knows those she can and cannot associate with by their caste. Quite often she is not free to choose her friends or her spouse. She, on the other hand, faces death without doubt of her immortality. She believes that she will return in another incarnation. On this point I have no hope of returning. My destiny is either heaven or hell. Each of these persons that I might have been, have very different belief structures— chiefly a result of the soul's choice of environment for this lifetime's experience.

> *The beliefs we hold are the guardians of our self-image and our identity.*

Thus, our acquired beliefs mostly depend on the society into which we are born. They derive their being from our sense of identity with the place and culture of our birth. Our identity, a composite of those factors in our environment to which we believe we belong, include nationality, race, religion and gender. They may also include class or caste, professional status, financial status, and roles we play— father, mother, son, daughter, protector, guardian, etc. As soon as we identify in any way, we immediately take on the beliefs that surround that identity. They become a set of clothes that cover our natural self. It is as if we have taken on a disguise that becomes the facade through which we deal with the world. The beliefs we hold are the guardians of our self-image and our identity.

Learned beliefs

We develop our learned beliefs through our interaction with others. In particular, relationships with parents, siblings, peers, and teachers strongly influence our beliefs. As we grow, we learn from these groups what is acceptable and unacceptable behavior. During the process, we allow ourselves to be molded through love bargains. We learn that certain types of behavior bring love, and other types of behavior bring punishment. For us to adopt the former and reject the latter is natural. Unknowingly we develop beliefs that help us avoid pain and gain pleasure. By the time we leave home, our belief structures about how we should relate to others are solidly built, and will influence our future relationships. However, the beliefs that we learned as children may not be valid when we become adults. In fact, they may be intensely dysfunctional and the cause of much unhappiness.

Let me give two examples. A mischievous child may get into trouble with parents or teachers. When that child is beaten and told by the parents that they administer punishment because they love him (or her), the child may unconsciously develop a belief that abuse can be an expression of love. This is a form of hypnosis that comes about through repeated suggestion. As an adult, he or she may grow up to beat children and perhaps their spouse, or even to become an adult victim of abuse.

A second example concerns children whose parents constantly tell them ,"You will never amount to anything." The children hear this so often that it becomes part of their unconscious beliefs. Later in life these people constantly disappoint themselves and others. The belief that they will not amount to much becomes a self-fulfilling prophecy.

The threads of these dysfunctional beliefs must be unraveled if you want to correct these situations in your life. You need to recognize that your beliefs create your reality. You must accept responsibility for what happens in your life. Your relationships mirror and reflect the full state of your consciousness. They reflect both the positive and negative parts of your personality and the owned (persona) and disowned (shadow) aspects of your psyche.

Self-inherited Beliefs

The least-recognized and yet most-dominant beliefs that condition our lives are those that come from past lives. They transcend time because they belong to the soul. Past life recall is a well-documented and a powerful psychotherapeutic tool currently practiced by a large number of therapists within the broad framework of transpersonal psychology. The fundamental difference between this branch of psychotherapy and other branches is the full recognition of the soul as part of our consciousness. Transpersonal psychology transcends the childhood complexes of the Freudian system, extends the Jungian theory of the collective unconscious and deals with the unfinished dramas of the soul left over from previous incarnations. But, as Roger Woolger points out in his authoritative account of past life regressions, it is not necessary to believe in reincarnation for past-life therapy to be effective.[1] All that is necessary is a belief common to all schools of psychotherapy—the healing power of the unconscious mind.

The principal tool in past-life therapy is regression. Most people today are familiar with the use of regression to access the forgotten traumas of childhood. Police use regression techniques combined with hypnotherapy to help witnesses recall evidence at the scene of a crime. Therapists repeatedly demonstrate that, by regressing their patients to an age when a violent or disturbing event took place, and having the patient relive the painful memories associated with the event, the memories can be assimilated in a new and broader perspective. The process of assimilation, called catharsis, brings an emotional release and a healing experience.

Past life therapy works in a similar way. Patients are simply asked to return to the moment in time when they first experienced the symptoms that cause them discomfort or pain. This process is aided by the verbal repetition of a phrase—a life metaphor

—representing a feeling associated with the problem. A life metaphor is a belief that encapsulates the emotion around a recurring, painful life situation.

When the regression gets underway, the patient spontaneously recounts stories dealing with the life metaphor. This may involve remembering childhood experiences from the present lifetime, or immediately recalling experiences from past lives. Those who remember experiences from this lifetime will almost always go on to recount experiences in past lives with the same theme. According to Woolger, 95 percent of people attending his workshops, or coming for treatment, are capable of experiencing past-life memories. To understand the relationship of past-life memories to beliefs let us look at a typical case history taken from Roger Woolger's *Other Lives, Other Selves*.

A woman who lived in a city apartment with her cats always felt anxious when she had to leave her cats, so much so that she hardly took vacations. Woolger recalls that, as he probed, there seemed to be all sorts of relationships with animals in her life that had disastrous outcomes. Two life metaphors began to appear in the conversation: *"I can't leave them, because something will happen to them,"* and, *"It's all my fault, I didn't do enough for them."* During the regression she began to tell a tearful story.

I'm an old woman living in a large bleak stone house. It's northern, maybe Scotland. There's a storm outside. I've been fighting with my husband. He says I don't care about the children. Perhaps he's right. I swore I'd never have children because I don't want to take care of them. But we've got two now, three and four years. He's outside screaming. I'm not letting him in. Let him take them if he knows better. I'm not letting them in. The storm's getting worse but he has stopped screaming now. It's quiet for a while, an hour or so. Now it's knocking, it sounds like my little boy. Oh, no he won't, he's not doing that one. He's just sent the boy because he thinks I'll relent. Well, I'll show him they are not coming in.

Now it's morning. The storm's over. They didn't come back. I'll bet they went to the inn. But I don't want to go to the door. Something's wrong. I go to the door finally; it won't open. Oh, my dear Lord. It's the children blocking it! My boy is unconscious, my husband's nowhere to be seen (she weeps bitterly). It's all my fault! It's all my fault! They must have been so scared out there, so weak and helpless! (deep sobbing and remorse).[2]

Woolger recounts that the rest of the story emerged slowly and painfully. The children died within hours. Her husband had loaded the children onto a handcart to go to the local inn. On the way, a storm arose and her husband collapsed and died of a heart attack. The children found their way back to tell their mother what had happened, only to be shut out by her. In her shame, the woman let her neighbors believe it was her husband's fault that the children died. Tormented by guilt the rest of her life, died with the thought, *"I don't trust myself to take care of anyone."* This was the story that lay behind her fear of leaving her cats. She gained much insight from this recollection and some time later overcame her anxiety.

You can discover your own life metaphors through self study, or a heart-to-heart discussion with a concerned friend. Simply spend time thinking about the times in your life when you have experienced severe discomfort or pain. Look for patterns in your reactions to situations. We all have life metaphors. Here are five that I have encountered amongst my friends. *I feel cheated. I feel a sense of loss. I feel people are holding back. I feel my life is concerned with trivia and I am missing out on the mainstream of activities. I feel discounted.* In all these cases, each person was able to identify several events in their lives that could be summarized by the wording of the life metaphor.

Previous incarnations not only affect our belief systems, they can also affect our physical body.

It is important to remember that life metaphors can be positive as well as negative. While we can learn a lot about ourselves from a study of positive life metaphors, it is by working with the negative metaphors that spiritual unfoldment and healing occur.

Life metaphors almost always derive from a memory experienced at the moment of death. Thoughts and feelings experienced at this moment are intense and become imprinted on the consciousness carried forward by the soul into other lives.

The transfer of a life metaphor takes place when the soul enters the fetus during pregnancy. We are thus born into the world with a psychic imprint. The beliefs we bring with us become the dominant themes in our life struggle.

The work of Ian Stevenson of the University of Virginia suggests that previous incarnations can also affect our physical bodies. Stevenson found numerous instances of physical injuries carrying over as scars or birthmarks. In some cases, with a clear recollection of the identity of the previous incarnation, he has found hospital or autopsy reports of the deceased personality which show that the injuries not only occurred, but were in the exact location of the present birthmark or deformity. Stevenson states,

> It seems to me that the imprint of wounds on the previous person-ality must be carried between lives on some kind of an extended body which in turn acts as a template for the production on a new physical body of birthmarks and deformities that correspond to the wounds of the body of the previous personality.[3]

Thus, we can see that both physical scars and mental scars can be carried forward into another life. This is not surprising since every cell of the body has a conscious awareness. A severe wound would mark the consciousness of the cell-mind just as a severe emotion would mark the consciousness of the soul-mind. Physical scars, or birthmarks, and past-life metaphors, both forms of emotional remembrance, transfer from one life to another through the mecha-nism of the soul.

The structure of beliefs

If you frequently encounter pain and discomfort in your life, then you can be sure there is a negative belief lurking in your mind. Some beliefs are so embedded in our unconscious that we are simply unaware of them. They have become hidden behind a pattern of emotional responses. The true trigger of the response, the belief system, is not recognized.

Your belief system is constructed like a building. Self-inherited beliefs are the foundations that thrust deep into the earth. They lie in the unconscious. These beliefs are difficult to access. The weight of the building rests upon them and hides them from view. Trying to change negative, self-inherited beliefs is painful, but like a bad tooth, the pain gets worse if not treated.

Learned beliefs form the main framework of the building. Some are structurally important, others less so. They can either lie in the conscious or unconscious. Accessing and changing learned beliefs can be painful if they are structurally important.

Acquired beliefs are the easiest to change. These represent the outer facade of the building. They can be modified and changed at will, without too much pain or difficulty. For example, many people change religious faiths several times in their lives.

Every day we create our reality through our beliefs. We do this in two ways—consciously and unconsciously. Most of the time we create our reality unconsciously. We do not recognize that our lives reflect our total consciousness. We see only what we want to see. We are prepared to take responsibility for the good things that happen to us, but fail to see that the bad things are also our responsibility. We can consciously create positive life situations when we release our unconscious, fear-based beliefs. As we do, we move into a state of soul consciousness. At this level of consciousness we become aware of our eternal nature and the power of unconditional love.

We cannot separate the healing of the individual from the healing of the planet. They are one and the same, because the consciousness of each individual is connected to the collective consciousness. Although we are individuals, we are also each part of the whole. Shakti Gawain

We have identified ourselves with our body, mind and personality, imagining these objects to constitute our real self and we then spend our entire lives trying to defend, protect, and prolong what is just an illusion. Ken Wilber

Be content with what you have; rejoice in the way things are. When you realize there is nothing lacking, the whole world belongs to you. Lao Tse

Others are merely mirrors of you. You cannot love or hate something about another person unless it reflects something you love or hate about yourself. Anonymous

7

Liberating the Soul

E very human being is the projection of an individual soul into three-dimensional consciousness. The true bearer of our individuality is the soul. By focusing its intention and concentrating its attention, the soul manifests itself in human form. The veil of three dimensional consciousness that divides us from our soul is one of a series of veils that lie between us and unity consciousness. Each veil of consciousness comprises a boundary of awareness. When we finally transcend these boundaries of consciousness during heightened states of awareness, we begin to get a broader perspective of our life here on earth.

Our physical body provides a vehicle for the manifestation of our soul, and our soul is the vehicle for the manifestation of God. In other words, the soul is God's idea manifested in a higher plane of consciousness, and we are the soul's idea manifested in the three-dimensional plane of consciousness. God infuses the soul with spirit that manifests as the will to live, the will to evolve, and the will to participate in the universal purpose. The secondary aspects of spirit are love and intelligence. Spirit is the life force and the universal energy present in all creation. Scientists find this same energy when they break down matter into its constituent parts.

The physical universe is a spontaneous exercise in creativity. As humans we learn in a three-dimensional context the ways in which we can use our consciousness to manifest our physical and psychic reality. We manipulate through our beliefs and thoughts the basic units of electro-magnetic energy to create situations and physical manifestations. Each thought and emotion is charged with energy. As we learn to control our emotions and thoughts, we consciously manifest and mold our reality. The intensity of the thought or emotion determines both the strength and the permanency of the physical result.

The earth, as a laboratory of the soul, exists as a place where souls can experience their creations. They experience, through the human form, intensities of emotion not available at higher levels of consciousness. For the soul, three-dimensional consciousness functions as an accelerated learning laboratory.

The soul perspective

Only when you recognize that you are a soul having a human experience can you can get a true perspective of life. Moving from a three-dimensional perspective to a four-dimensional perspective represents a major leap in understanding. Such an understanding is important because the principles governing four-dimensional consciousness also govern the human mind. Integrating the fourth-dimensional perspective into your daily life brings your personality into alignment with your soul. You then experience joy, love, harmony, and peace on a continual and renewing basis.

Compared to the third dimension of consciousness, the fourth dimension exists as a timeless, spaceless, energy-based reality. Timeless because of the pervasive sense of the present moment, there are no memories of the past or thoughts of the future. We can attain this state in three-dimensional consciousness by being truly mindful of every moment. Unfortunately, in three-dimensional conscious-ness, we usually have allow fear and anger to enter into our reality. Anger is the memory of past pain revisited; fear is the memory of past pain projected into the future. Pain, an energy imbalance caused by the lack of attunement of the personality's beliefs with those of the soul, occurs when the low vibrational fear energy of the ego meets the high vibrational love energy of the soul. As soon as we allow fear into our mind, our awareness becomes distracted from the present moment. We project the pain of the past into the future and set in motion fear-based thought patterns. At this point we no longer experience just being.

Anger has the same effect. We become focused on what happened in the past and the object of our anger. Our anger is really with ourselves and about our own lack of attunement. Behind our anger resides a feeling of not being cared for. Behind that resides a belief that we are not loved. Anger projects onto the outside world the guilt we feel about our own lack of oneness with our soul. We project it onto

Anger is a symptom of the ego's denial of responsibility, and lack of attunement with the soul.

an outside object or person because we cannot bear the guilt of the separation we have created from our soul. Anger is a symptom of the ego's denial of responsibility for its lack of attunement with the soul and is based on fear.[1]

When we allow anger and fear into our mind, we shut out awareness of the present moment. We either relive past experiences with the emotion of anger, or anticipate future experiences with the emotion of fear. However, whether we experience anger or fear, we still experience it in the present moment. Our awareness becomes clogged with memories or projections and denies us the pleasure of just being. Learning to live in the now, outside anger and fear, is an important step in learning to experience the soul dimension of consciousness.

The fourth dimension of consciousness is spaceless in the sense that all energy interchanges and communications are instantaneous. This is achieved through telepathy. Telepathic exchanges occur so fast that they defy our three-dimensional understanding of space. Our modern communications systems do the same. It is possible to have a conversation with someone by telephone at the opposite end of the globe and yet have the feeling that they are in an adjacent room. The speed at which the energy of the voice transmits defies our senses. The more you believe in the three-dimensional illusion of

separation, the more difficult it is for you to receive or send telepathic communications.

The energy aspect of life is now well documented. Attempts to
break the atom have yielded only energy. There are no basic physical
building blocks for our material world. Objects and matter exist as
energy forms held together by forces of attraction. Our bodies are
energy forms created by our souls. When we die, the organizing
principle leaves our physical body and the body disintegrates into
lower forms of energy groupings that make up the basic chemical
elements. Our thoughts are also energy forms. When supported by
intense beliefs and vision, they have the power to change the
characteristics of existing physical energy forms and manifest new
realities.

When we become aware of universal energy, we see that we are
connected to all things. The energy that flows through our being is
the same energy that flows through everything. Consider for a
moment all creation as a river and the water in the river as universal
energy. In some places the water flows rapidly and in other places it
flows slowly; the river can be turbulent or calm, with eddies or -
whirlpools. The form the water takes depends upon the shape of the
river bed and the banks. We can see the forms in the river, but we
cannot see what causes these forms. Our souls are similar to the
forces that cause eddies and whirlpools in the river. They give form
to the universal energy but cannot be seen. We as humans, like the
eddies and whirlpools in the river, have a form that was created by
our soul, and that form expresses itself through universal energy.

The more we recognize time, space, and matter as properties of
our three-dimensional perception, the more we open ourselves to the
timeless, spaceless, energy world of the fourth dimension. We must
learn to ignore the illusion of our physical senses if we want to live
in the fourth dimension. Compared to three-dimensional consciousness characterized by death, decay, and separation, the fourth
dimension continues as a constantly evolving flux of energy and
being.

The soul experiences life vastly different from that of a human.
Aware of the timeless dimension of its existence and its connection

through the mind to all other souls, the soul is aware only of love. The energy we call fear is of such low vibrational frequency that it cannot exist in the higher realms of consciousness. The soul knows complete freedom and does not discriminate between souls. This freedom and equality are God given. The experience of the soul is one of everlasting life, connection, love, freedom, and equality. The soul desires unity consciousness—a state of complete oneness with all creation.

To assist our souls in their evolution, we need to embrace the concept of unity consciousness and bring it into all aspects of our lives. As humans, we all share a set of primary beliefs which reflect the nature of our souls. These beliefs express themselves in our lives as basic needs. The soul experience of eternal life transfers to humans as reverence for life and the need to live. The soul experience of connection transfers to humans as the need to belong, or to be part of something greater than ourselves. The soul experience of oneness expresses as the human need to love and be loved. The soul experience of freedom expresses as the need to feel responsible for ourselves, for it is only through freedom that responsibility can be exercised. The soul experience of equality creates the human need for justice.

Stop for a moment and ask yourself the following questions. Why do we feel the need to belong? Why do we feel the need to love and be loved? Why do we feel the need to be responsible? Why do we feel the need for justice? For some reason we all share a common perspective among these particular sets of needs, and yet there is no intrinsic reason why we should feel so inclined, unless they reflect a

All experiences in the human condition serve the soul in its purpose of reaching unity consciousness.

common unconscious heritage—the heritage of the soul. In reality our subconscious minds are laden with soul memories and beliefs. Very often we become aware of them only through the causes we defend, our general attitudes, and our behavior. Deep in our unconscious lie the aspirations of our soul.

All experiences in the human condition are designed by the soul to serve the purpose of reaching unity consciousness. By learning to love unconditionally we reach this goal. Our limited three-dimensional perception represents a major stumbling block to achieving unity consciousness. Time, space, and matter impact on our belief systems to such an extent that we no longer are aware of the unity of all things and our connection to all aspects of creation. We have become lost in three-dimensional consciousness; we see fragmentation, not connection. When we perceive only fragmentation, we live in fear and anger. When we practice the principles of unity, we find love, joy, and peace. To overcome our beliefs in separation, we must tackle the problem at four levels.

Levels of fragmentation

As souls, we were given two wondrous gifts: the power to create, and free will. Using the energy we call spirit souls created the living forms we see on our planet. They became so involved in their creation that they forgot their true identity. They objectified God, forgetting that they are part of God. This is the first level of mind fragmentation and the major issue of the soul.

During the human experience the soul became involved with three further levels of fragmentation: the separation of the human organism from its environment; the separation of our mind from our body; and the separation of our shadow from our persona. [2,3] These three levels of fragmentation are the root causes of the environmental degradation of our planet, the sickness of our bodies, and our dysfunctional relationships. Healing must occur at all these levels before the soul can attain unity consciousness.

Separation of humanity from the planet. We experience the first level of fragmentation as the distinction between the human organism and our natural environment. We see ourselves separate from the world of nature. Our whole attitude to the natural world is that we want to dominate it, control it, and use it for our benefit. We do not care about the flora and fauna, the forests, oceans and wetlands because we do not identify with the natural world. The last thing modern society thinks about is living in harmony with its natural surroundings. We do not realize that everything else on the planet is a projection from the fourth dimension of consciousness. Just as we are the projection of our souls, everything on the planet is the projection of other souls that have chosen to manifest themselves in different ways. The souls responsible for other forms of life are part of the same creation and connected through the same energy system to all there is. In other words, the world and everything in it forms part of a collective cooperative consciousness system similar to our own bodies. Just as the different parts of your body work together for the good of the whole, the planet depends on the different aspects of the natural world for its survival.

When we identify only with our own organism, we fail to see our connection with the rest of creation. We develop a dysfunctional relationship with the souls of nature. Healing at this level of separation occurs as we remember our oneness with every other aspect of soul consciousness that forms part of our planet. This is about healing the fragmentation that has occurred between our human organism and the rest of creation. As we recognize our connection to all creation, we will accept responsibility for the stewardship of the Earth.

Separation of mind from body. We experience the second level of fragmentation as the distinction between our mind and our body. We see our body and our mind as separate, not part of an integrated whole. We do not realize that our beliefs, emotions, attitudes, and thoughts affect our body's health. When systems are categorized and broken down into smaller and smaller parts, we lose the big picture and miss the connectivity of the whole. We make assumptions to patch over the cracks in our knowledge system and believe them to be the truth.

The belief in our body's vulnerability to external attack opens us to the possibility of disease and suffering. With such a belief we immediately enter into a dysfunctional relationship with our body and the external world. In reality, our bodies physically express the energy field of our soul. Healing at this level of separation is about remembering the wholeness of our being. It is about healing the fragmentation that has occurred between our mind and our body. As we recognize this connection, and we accept responsibility for the health of our body, we begin to heal ourselves. We do this by releasing the fears that create sickness and disease.

Separation of our shadow from our persona. We experience the third level of fragmentation as the distinction between our persona (the aspects of consciousness we own) and our shadow (the aspects of our consciousness we disown). All those aspects of our personality that we are not comfortable with, or feel guilty about, we deny. They become part of our shadow. The only way we can identify them is by seeing them in other people. When we get angry or upset and begin to make judgments about others, then we must pay attention be-

> *Pollution, sickness, and dysfunctional relationships are all symbolic reflections of the breakdown of communication between the fragmented parts of our being.*

cause those judgments comprise about the aspects of our personality that we have denied. The world we see outside of ourselves reflects our inner consciousness in all its detail. The angry judgments we make are aspects of our shadow projecting themselves into the world. Whenever you hear yourself or someone else criticizing, listen carefully because they are talking about their own issues. Thus, if we only identify with our persona and do not integrate the content of our shadow, we separate ourselves from others by the judgments we make of them. This creates dysfunctional relationships. Healing at this level of separation is about reidentifying with the hidden aspects of our psyche. As we learn to accept ourselves the way we truly are, warts and all, we begin to accept responsibility for our relationships.

Healing the mind
Pollution, sickness, and dysfunctional relationships all symbolically reflect the breakdown of communication between the fragmented parts of our being. As we heal the fragmentation that has occurred

in our "human mind," we raise the level of conscious awareness of our "soul-mind." As we accept responsibility for the creation of our reality, we enter into a symbiotic relationship with the natural world, with our bodies, and with others around us. Environmental pollution, physical pain, and emotional discomfort all remind us of the fragmentation of consciousness that has occurred in our minds. They reflect our lack of identification with the forgotten aspects of our selves. When we identify, the object of our identification becomes part of whom we are. We enter into a relationship with it. When we begin to identify with someone, we start to care for them and learn through dialogue how they perceive and understand the world. When we identify with our body, we begin to care for it and nourish it. When we identify with our environment, the earth, the plants, the animals, and birds, we begin to care for them and learn to respect all life. Through this process of reconnection we get in touch with the fragmented parts of our greater self and we become a whole. This is the true meaning of healing.

The purpose of our being here on earth is to become whole, to release our beliefs in separation and achieve unity consciousness. We do this by embracing unconditional love. That, in a nutshell, is what we are here to do. This is the service we render to our soul. *A Course in Miracles* puts it very succinctly, "This is a course in miracles. It is a required course. Only the time you take it is voluntary."[4] In other words, we are here on earth to prepare ourselves for living in unity consciousness. We can take as many incarnations as we like to learn our lessons. The faster we learn to embrace unconditional love, the quicker we reach unity consciousness. This involves permanently lifting the veil of three-dimensional consciousness so that we become aware of our larger reality.

Our purpose here in the physical dimension of consciousness is to help our souls evolve to unity consciousness. We do this by creating a life for our soul. As we bring our personality and soul into alignment, we create the conditions through which our soul can live out its purpose. We find joy and meaning in our life as we implement this purpose.

At some point in time, our souls will decide they have nothing left to learn from earth experiences and will decide not to reincarnate. They will move into other dimensions of consciousness. In these higher realms, they will work at healing the separation that exists between the soul and other realms of the universe (cosmic consciousness), the separation between the soul as the universe and God (God consciousness), and finally, the separation between the soul as God, and the total unity of everything (unity consciousness). At this level the soul will no longer objectify God, but become at one with all there is. For most of us this level of consciousness is still a long way away. This does not mean we should sit back and do nothing. On the contrary, this is a journey that we are destined to make. Better to make an early start rather than leave it until later.

Part Two
Transformation

I have treated many hundreds of patients. Among those in the second half of their life—that is to say over thirty-five—there has not been one whose problem, in the last resort, was not that of finding a religious outlook on life.
Carl Jung

Life should be giving birth to the soul, the development of a higher mode of reality, the blind, greedy, selfish nature of man must put on beauty and nobleness. This heavenly alchemy is what justifies our presence on the earth; this is our mission and our glory. Henri Frederic Amiel

You will not grow if you sit in a beautiful flower garden, but you will grow if you are sick, if you are in pain, if you experience losses, and if you do not put your head in the sand, but take the pain and learn to accept it, not as a curse or a punishment but as a gift to you with a very, very specific purpose. Elizabeth Kubler-Ross

We always attract into our lives whatever we think about the most, believe in most strongly, expect on the deepest level, and/or imagine most vividly. Shakti Gawan

Reality is unchanging but your perception of reality changes as you change. The difference before and after enlightenment, therefore, is in you—not in reality. John White

8

The Process of Unfoldment

Up to this point, our focus has been on the importance of self-knowledge. We attempted to address the question "Who am I?" by developing and discussing a multidimensional model of reality that incorporates higher dimensions of consciousness. We saw that human experience is contained within soul experience. We all are souls having a human experience. Our true reality lies in a higher dimension of consciousness. For the soul, the human form provides an intense learning experience. When you are able to identify with your soul you can consciously contribute to the learning experience. Until you do this, it will seem as if you are lost in a maze. You will have only a vague idea about life's purpose. The way you find your way initially is by building upon the belief systems you assumed from your parents. As time passes, you will modify your belief systems based upon your life experiences.

A-mazing life
Despite extreme diversity of backgrounds, the majority of humans spend their lives seeking to achieve one primary goal—that of happiness. This represents the center of the maze for most people. In searching for happiness we also spend much time and energy trying to avoid pain.

The maze of life is about making choices. The choices we make are all somehow conditioned by our search for happiness and our aversion to pain. In the early years of our lives, we move from one experience to another, making choices that maximize short-term personal pleasure. We allow our beliefs to mechanically control the direction of our life journey. As time goes by, we find that some of the choices made in the search for happiness actually caused us pain. We begin to realize that happiness eludes us more than we first imaged.

In my own life, I remember searching for happiness through status, money, and my relationship with a significant other. Things would go well for some time, but then suddenly I would encounter a painful situation. It was as if I turned a corner of the maze that I thought lead to happiness and I ran into a brick wall. Having steadied myself, I would think things through and vow not to repeat that choice again. But, to my intense humiliation, I repeated the same mistake, with an equally painful result. I began to realize that it was my belief about the path to happiness that was my problem. Somehow, the beliefs that guided my life choices were faulty. They were leading me down pathways of pain. My revelations came to me in three parts.

First, I learned that the subconscious belief I had about living my life to fulfill the wishes and goals of others simply did not work. My father, who died when I was 17, had always instilled in me the importance of going to college and getting a good job—something that had been denied to him and everyone else in my family. Subconsciously, I drove myself to do well for his sake. I graduated with honors and became a successful consulting engineer in a large international company. I was the youngest associate of the firm, and the one chosen to open a new office in Paris. Everyone viewed me as very successful. Despite all this approbation, I felt empty inside. I knew I was not being true to myself. I was not expressing who I really was. I was living my life to please others. I knew I had to go back to the place where I had entered the maze, a little older and wiser, and begin again. I gave up my executive position to work on my own as an independent consultant.

Working on my own, with no superiors to please, or peers to impress, I began to find myself and my own path to happiness. I began to see the shallowness of the status I had been seeking and the fear that had been driving my ambition. I had used status and the fruits of ambition for my self-esteem. The reason I felt empty inside was because my self-worth derived from external sources rather than internal. This made me totally dependent on others for how I felt about myself. I had ransomed my soul for the approval of others. Working outside of any supporting hierarchy, I could find out what was pleasing to me. My work ethic changed. From being driven to seek external praise and recognition, I began to seek internal meaning. Before, I used to put my energies into giving to others to receive praise in return. I was now able to give unconditionally. I realized that my job was to take care of my client's needs, not my own. Through this process I became my own person. No longer dependent on others for my self-esteem, I was now ready to move back into a large organization. I was operating from a source of internal power and did not need the organization. The organization needed me. When I could no longer satisfy my goals through the work the organization offered me, then it would be time to move on. This was liberating because it gave me the ability to operate with integrity and outside of fear.

My second revelation was the same as the first, but this time it applied to my relationship with a significant other. I depended on her approval and her happiness for my own. I was so needy of

The route to personal happiness is not through serving self, but through serving others.

love that I could not be my true self. My love was conditional. The condition to my giving love was that I receive love in return. Such giving has only one outcome—pain—and places an intolerable burden on the relationship.

I learned through these experiences that successful relationships, at work and at home, are based on similar principles. The route to personal happiness in relationships is not through serving self, but through serving others. Listening and responding to the needs of the other affirms the relationship. Focusing on giving rather than receiving was the path I needed to follow. The belief that I had needs and that these needs could only be satisfied by someone else was the cause of my pain and suffering.

At about this time, I began to suspect that my beliefs were creating my reality and that the happiness I was seeking could not be found in the external world. This caused me to turn inward in my search for the path to the center of the maze. I began to realize that my real quest was for self-knowledge. I did not know who I really was, nor was I sure how I created my reality.

I began to explore my inner world by learning to meditate. I took this on with the same fervor I had when I explored my outer world. I discovered through meditation that I could access my soul. As I continued my daily meditation, I found increasingly lengthy periods of peace and joy in my life.

Lived to its full, life is not an external journey in search of happiness, but an internal journey in search of meaning.

My goal became making this experience permanent, not just something to feel when sitting in the quiet of my own room, but something that permeated my everyday experiences and relationships. For the first time in my life I understood the difference between happiness and joy. I learned that joy is a deep, lasting inner experience felt when the personality attunes with the soul. I learned that happiness is a short-lived experience that occurs when our perceived needs are satisfied, either through material possessions, relationships, or personal success. Happiness is an internal reaction to an external experience. Joy is an internal reaction to an internal state of being. That state of being is nothing less than the attunement of the personality with the soul. Beyond joy lies bliss. Bliss is the experience of soul as it embraces unity consciousness.

My last revelation was that my mind was, in large measure, controlled by my unconscious beliefs. My thoughts and my behavior had been the offspring of these unconscious beliefs. I realized that I was not really in control of my life. I was unconsciously creating my experience of life by interpreting events through the filters of my beliefs. Suddenly, I was no longer a victim of others, but a victim of my own belief system. I was giving every event in my life all the meaning it had for me through my beliefs. What a revelation to me. I realized that if I changed the way I looked at things—changed my beliefs—then I could change my experience of reality.

The treasure that lies at the center of the maze is not happiness but the experience of soul. The peace, freedom, joy, and love that we constantly search for already exists at the core of our being. We need look no further than our soul. Thus, lived fully, life is not an external journey in search of happiness, but an internal journey in search of meaning. The emotions that external events release in us mirror our beliefs. The more we embrace our soul and the operational principles of the fourth dimension of consciousness, the more those beliefs reflect love. The path of self-knowledge is the path that leads to the recovery of the soul.

A-mazing lessons

The analogy of life as a maze is full of interesting metaphors. First, you must be aware that you are *in* a maze, and that a treasure awaits you at the center. Without this awareness, you have no incentive to attain self-knowledge. You will wander through life aimlessly, ending it just as far from happiness as when you began. Beginning the journey of recovering your soul requires two conditions. You must have faith that things can improve. Without faith, the maze will become a labrynth of despair. The second condition requires that you accept the situation you find yourself in at the start of the journey. If you feel you are life's victim, or unfairly treated in any way, you will get stuck in your anger. Remember that your soul chose the circumstances and conditions surrounding your birth, and it did so with a purpose in mind. By railing against these starting conditions you are railing against your soul. Without acceptance you will live in bitterness and find no meaning in your journey. You will be at odds with your soul.

When your beliefs encompass faith and acceptance, only then are you ready to move forward. Your task is to discover the operation rules of the maze so that you can maximize joy, freedom, peace, and love and minimize pain, suffering, and despair. You begin to move forward using the best instructions you can find. These may come from religious beliefs, your parents, or the values of your society. As you come to branches in the maze (forks in the road), you will have to make choices. Some choices may lead you into painful situations. Others will bring happiness. Whatever transpires from the choices you make, you must accept responsibility for the results. Your beliefs (about the pathway to the center) guide you in making choices. You decide which way to go, even if you make such choices unconsciously. As you accept responsibility for your choices, you begin to see patterns forming. Certain beliefs

Pain and emotional discomfort have nothing to do with God's punishment. They are the result of an energy dynamic that reflects the lack of attunement of your personality with your soul.

bring painful situations; other beliefs make your journey smooth. The maze seems to provide you feedback based on the beliefs that govern your choices. The more your choices embrace unity the more "right" they are. The more your choices embrace separation the more "wrong" they are. Gradually, you attune to the principles that govern the operation of the maze. As you begin to integrate these principles into your life, your journey becomes easier.

Pain is our helper in this process. If we did not have pain, we would not be able to attune with our soul. Pain is a signal that tells us when we are not attuned. As a light on the dashboard of life, it flashes when you move out of alignment with your soul. Whenever you feel any form of emotional discomfort, you can be sure that you have found an issue separating you from your soul. Behind this discomfort or pain lies a false belief about reality. At the heart of that false belief lies fear.

When you find yourself repeatedly experiencing the same discomfort and pain, then be sure that you have discovered a fear-based belief that you need to release. The pain and discomfort tell you to reexamine your beliefs. Welcome them as signposts prompting you to make different choices. Understand this—pain and discomfort have nothing to do with God's punishment. They are the result of an energy dynamic that reflects your personality's lack of attunement with your soul. The lack of attunement begins as discomfort in the mind and can eventually manifest itself as pain and sickness in the body. These pain and discomfort signposts help us identify the beliefs that are sabotaging our lives. They are a consequence of wrong-thinking and signposts to right-thinking. They are positive experiences: welcome them. Unfoldment and attunement proceed as you release the fear beliefs causing your discomfort and pain.

Finally, it is important to emphasize the importance of raising your awareness. Meditation gives us direct access to the soul. As you raise your awareness, your consciousness lifts beyond the three-dimensional world with which we normally associate ourselves to the realm of the soul. You attain a new perspective beyond physical reality. In the fourth and higher dimensions of consciousness you move beyond space and time into the realm of the soul.

The journey of unfoldment begins with faith and acceptance. It involves taking full responsibility for your choices, searching for meaning in your experiences, welcoming pain and discomfort as positive feedback, modifying your beliefs by releasing your fears, discovering the principles that bring joy and peace, and integrating these principles into your daily life. If you want your unfoldment to proceed quickly and smoothly, then practice raising your awareness to higher levels of consciousness every day.

*It is not possible to tell men what way they should take . . .
Everyone should carefully observe what way his heart draws him
to, and follow this way with all his strength.* Seer of Lublin

*Come to the edge, he said. They said: we are afraid. Come to the
edge he said. They came . . . He pushed them . . . and they flew.*
Guillaume Apollinaire

The good life is to live on honorable terms with your own soul.
Saul Bellow

*We are members of a vast cosmic orchestra in which each living
instrument is essential, complimentary and harmonious to the
playing of the whole.* Allan Boone

No snowflake ever falls in the wrong place. Zen saying

*No one is where he is by accident, and chance plays no part in
God's plan. A Course in Miracles*

9

What Did I Come Here to Do?

The soul has two primary motives for taking physical form. First, it seeks to learn specific lessons to facilitate its own development toward unity consciousness. To do this, it assumes a personality that reflects its own state of evolution. The personality becomes the agent of the soul in the third dimension of consciousness. The process of unfoldment occurs as the personality aligns with values that reflect unity consciousness.

Second, every soul brings a unique gift, a contribution to the common good that reflects some aspect of unity consciousness. It may be nurturing children, caring for the elderly, sick, or infirm, seeking to improve conditions for other species, or furthering our understanding of the physical world. This contribution is often called the soul's purpose. The scope of the purpose may be large or small; it may involve supporting another human being, or assisting thousands. Whatever it is, it will involve some form of service to the human race or to planet Earth.

You may not be specifically aware of your soul purpose, but you probably recognize certain activities from which you derive immense satisfaction. Over the length of your life you may find yourself getting involved in many different types of service, or you may find yourself being drawn to express yourself in one particular way. If you want to find your soul's purpose, search for those experiences that give you the most satisfaction. Whatever provides you an inner sense of fulfillment will be closely linked to your soul purpose. Very often we know our soul purpose, but do not want to acknowledge it because it does not correspond with our chosen career or the identity we carefully cultivated for ourselves.

The form and size of the gift you bring as a soul is not important. What *is* important is that you give your gift *unconditionally*. The offering of this gift is the service you bring to humanity. Whatever gift you have to offer, there will be someone who needs it. As individual cells in the

We all have a responsibility to care for humanity and planet Earth. Giving service is the way you acknowledge that responsibility.

body of human consciousness, we all have a particular role to perform. It is important for the good of the whole that we play our role. The whole of nature works on this principle. If you look closely at a beehive or a termite mound, you will find particular groups of bees or termites with specific roles. They play out those roles for the common good. The hive of bees and the mound of termites represent a unity where each individual has a role to play. When you look in a broader sense at particular ecosystems such as the African savanna or swamplands, you find groups of animals, birds, insects and plants, each with specific roles to play in maintaining the harmony of the whole. We, as souls, have a responsibility to care for humanity and planet Earth. Giving your gift of service is the way you acknowledge that responsibility.

Very often the contribution you are able to make to the good of the whole is conditioned by the progress you make in personal unfoldment. When your lessons are hard, you become preoccupied with your own pain and suffering. You feel like you have little energy available to help others. Your survival is your primary concern. In short, you find it difficult to focus on giving your gift until you have lightened your own burden. It behooves each one of us, therefore, to recognize that progress in personal unfoldment is necessary if we are to fully participate as a server of humanity. Before we can fully focus on the needs of others, we need to be free of the fears that preoccupy our minds.

Finding your purpose

Some people discover their purpose early in life, while others discover it much later. The story of Bess provides an example of someone who came to understand her purpose late in life. When Bess came to seek my help, the first thing she said was that she did not know why she had come. At first, I could not understand either. Sitting before me was a woman full of vitality with an appearance that belied her age. She clearly was living a spiritually rich life.

She soon confided in me that she was not sure of her purpose. She did not know what she should be doing with her life. She and her husband were comfortably retired and lived in very pleasant surroundings. They were active members of the local golf club, but Bess felt disconnected from the social milieu that provided no fulfillment or satisfaction.

The next issue Bess raised was the fear she felt every day on awakening. This had been going on for years. We began by exploring the past. Bess was a diplomat's daughter, and throughout her childhood she had lived in countries with civil disturbances. She learned at a very young age that the world could be a very dangerous place in which to live.

Using guided imagery, I directed her to a peaceful place in the countryside. I had her discover a treasure box hidden in the bushes. Inside the box was a gift from her soul that would have an important bearing on her problem. I asked her to open the box. To our surprise, she found a golden-haired child inside the box. She instantly recognized the child as herself and she was afraid to come out of the box. I told her to encourage the child to come out and to tell her that there was no longer any danger. She could safely venture out into the outside world now. A smile of joy appeared on Bess's face as the child came out of the box. She had recovered a lost part of herself that had been afraid of the outside world. The fear that Bess had experienced for years when waking disappeared completely.

We focused Bess's second visit on releasing the accumulated negative energy of her fears and building her confidence. We did not talk about her purpose, although I suggested she might like to consider working as a volunteer with a charity that I was helping to organize. Although I did not know it at that time, my suggestion put her on the spot because it confronted her with a decision of whether to help me or find her own purpose. It was exactly what she needed. Confronted with a specific proposal forced her to evaluate what she really wanted to do.

She walked in beaming at the next visit. I knew something had happened. She told me that she now knew her purpose. She had been forced to make a choice, and her unconscious had delivered her a message that her purpose was to support her family. She felt this as a deep truth. However, that was not all. She then told me that she composed poetry and songs, and she wanted me to hear them. She sat reading and singing to me for half an hour. The inspiring poetry and beautiful songs had deep meaning. They clearly came from her soul. I found that she trained as a singer when young, but had subsequently lost interest in music. Only recently had she started writing her own songs and singing them, but she never sang them in public. I told her how easy it was to tape in a recording studio and invited her to sing at an upcoming workshop I was giving in our local area. I knew her songs would make a beautiful prelude to my guided meditations. She agreed instantly. Two weeks later she wrote to me saying she had gone home from her last visit and immediately written some new songs. In addition she had been to the recording studio and had made a tape.

This latent and dormant talent was a gift truly worth sharing. It gave meaning to Bess's life and pleasure to all who heard her sing. She simply needed to overcome the fear of exposing her soul.

Whenever the time comes in your life that you feel an inner need to fulfill yourself, you need to pay attention. The awareness of this need may be felt as dissatisfaction with work, or it may take the form of a crisis of meaning—a realization that what you are doing does not align with your inner values. This inner turbulence is your soul purpose bubbling up into your consciousness. If the turbulence is not acknowledged or integrated, it will find another way to attract your attention. The more you resist it the greater will be its impact on your well being. You will become increasingly unhappy, or even depressed. You may attribute the cause of your unhappiness to the outside world by blaming your discomfort on your spouse, lover, colleagues or family. You can be sure that the cause is *not* external. Your inner values are simply misaligned with your outer experience. Your depression is caused by anger at yourself. Whenever you feel discomfort, frustration, pain, or suffering, your personality is no longer aligned with your soul.

Finding your soul purpose and living it out is the greatest gift you can give yourself and others. Choosing to follow your soul purpose leads you to soul consciousness. For those well established in their careers, the pathway to soul consciousness can sometimes mean making painful choices. You may feel the need to give up your career and start anew, or alternately, you may find your happiness by bringing spiritual values into your workplace.

Moving from career to mission

Merely contemplating these changes will probably bring up fears and doubts in your mind. When you speak of them to your spouse or colleagues, unless they are on a spiritual path themselves, it is unlikely they will understand. They are more likely to try to dissuade you from continuing on this path. Their first and natural reaction will be a fear of what it might mean to their own security. Eventually you may face a conflict between your need to follow your own inner voice and the resistance posed by others around you. There is little you can do other than assure them of your unconditional love and ask for their faith and trust. If their fears do not permit their unconditional love, you may have to make the painful decision of going ahead without their support. If such decisions are needed, be *sure* that you are listening to your soul. If your calling primarily brings benefits to you, then it may simply be your ego demanding that its desires be met. If on the other hand, your calling focuses on service to others, or to the planet, then you are very likely listening to the voice of your soul. You will know intuitively what is true.

When I first began to recognize what my soul was calling me to do, it seemed as if my career and my mission were pulling me in opposite directions. I felt torn apart and could not see how to integrate practical spirituality into my career. About this time, I sought the advice of a respected friend in England who had experienced a similar transformation experience. He saw no conflict with my mission of helping people to live in soul consciousness and at the same time my working at the World Bank. "On the contrary," he said, "that is probably the best place for you to give your gift." The more I thought about his words, the more I realized

When you accept the challenge to implement your soul's purpose, you will be moving from career to mission.

he was right. I already recognized that there is an overwhelming need for our society to bring spiritual values into the workplace. When I opened myself up to that idea, I began to see how it might be possible. The universe responded appropriately by presenting me with the opportunity of creating a Spiritual Unfoldment Society in the World Bank. I became an agent for change in the workplace, bringing together my professional and spiritual interests.

For anyone experiencing a similar dilemma, let me *encourage* you to integrate your spiritual journey into your working life. There is a great need to bring spiritual values into the corporate setting, either by providing a forum for people to meet and discuss spiritual matters, or persuading your organization to shift from a paradigm of competition, exploitation, and self-interest, to cooperation, empowerment, and the common good.

When you accept the challenge to implement your soul's purpose, you will soon move from career to mission. You will need to become fearless and disciplined. Soul work cannot be undertaken half heartedly; it demands total commitment. This commitment does *not* require you to become a workaholic. On the contrary, soul work is joyful and light. Advanced soul workers do not labor hard to achieve results. They manifest what they want to create through the power of their minds and by understanding the principles of manifestation. This does not mean you can simply sit back and make things happen through the power of your thoughts. You have to put physical energy into what you do. You must create a vision of what it is you want to achieve. This can be your vision for your future or, if you are involved with others, it could be a group vision. The strength of the vision and its intent to contribute to the common good enables soul workers to manifest easily.

Above all else, soul workers understand the use of energy. They never engage in headlong combat. They work in cooperation rather than competition, with love rather than fear, searching always for the common good rather than personal gain. When they meet resistance, they conserve their energy by searching out parallel paths. They also know how to work with time. They avoid the fear that surrounds arbitrarily constructed deadlines by keeping themselves flexible and open to opportunities. Wherever there is fear, there is constriction. Fear prevents the manifestation of vision. When we constrain life, we kill spontaneity and cut off opportunities. By removing fear from our lives, we achieve our goals faster and often in a different way than expected.

Caring for yourself

The soul recognizes that the strength you give to its purpose requires you to be strong. For you to remain strong, you must learn to care for yourself. Soul workers know how to care for themselves. They frequently take rests, making sure they care for the mind, body, and soul and they work with concentration and purpose. Caring for yourself is one of the most essential requirements for you as a soul worker. If you are not strong yourself, it is unlikely that you will be able to help others.

Discipline, too, is important, not in the military sense, but in the sense of finding a time and place to care for *all* your needs. You need a time for yourself and time to be with others. You need a time for meditation and prayer, and a time for exercise. Avoid asceticism and excesses in all their forms. Developing this inner attitude of discipline is one of the most difficult challenges we face. Our egos are conditioned to serve our desire for pleasure rather than our real needs. The soul calls us on this journey, not our ego. The ego finds all sorts of excuses to skip meditation or exercise. It is a difficult struggle to convince the ego that by giving service it can move from pleasure to joy. When you encounter the ego's resistance, immediately become an observer of your consciousness. Say to yourself: there goes my ego again, wanting its luxuries and pleasures. Do not be hard on yourself, but be persistent. Above all, learn to listen to your soul.

Communicating with your soul

Whenever my soul spoke to me and I listened, I found myself engaged in a life-changing event. Sometimes it was my life that changed, sometimes it was the lives of others, sometimes it was both. Every time I accepted the call, I moved my faith forward.

On the first four occasions I heard the call of my soul, I had significant doubts. Every fear I could think of visited me. I doubted my own abilities; I doubted the acceptance of my ideas by others; and I doubted I could raise the funds necessary to implement my plans. These doubts and fears were my limiting beliefs. They measured my lack of faith and trust in my own soul. Through these experiences I learned to trust my soul and its connections with the rest of the universe. Now when I hear the inner voice, I trust it immediately. If I have any doubts at all, I ask for a sign. The sign never takes long to appear.

Late in 1992, after I shared some of the concepts of this book with a group of colleagues in the World Bank, the idea unfolded for setting up some form of World Bank spiritual study group. As I explained earlier, I had been seeking opportunities to bring my mission and my career into alignment. Bringing together this group to discuss the concepts of this book was a starting point toward achieving this goal. A few weeks after we discussed my book, I changed jobs within the organization. The challenge of the new job was daunting. After one month in my new position, two friends from the discussion group approached me and asked if I would set up the spiritual study group. I said I would think about it, but decided that it would take too much time. I thought it would distract me from meeting the challenges of my new job. However, knowing how the soul works, I decided to ask for help. I offered a prayer by simply saying to my soul, if you want me to do this, give me a sign.

A few days later I received a call from a lady I did not know. She and her friend both worked in the World Bank and had seen my picture in a newsletter. The corresponding article discussed a seminar I had given on *Liberating the Soul* to a meeting of the Association for Research and Enlightenment in South Africa. They asked me to set up some form of spiritual study group at the World Bank. I smiled inwardly because here was my sign. We met. I explained that I was willing to set up the group, but that I had little time to devote to the administrative aspects. They told me not to worry about that because they would take care of whatever had to be done. "Just tell us what to do and we will do it," was their response. My prayer had been answered with full acknowledgment of my concerns.

That was the start of the Spiritual Unfoldment Society (SUS). We announced the venture in a weekly staff bulletin and within a short time set up a steering committee. We decided to meet every Wednesday lunch time for one hour. Attendance grew rapidly. In three months the meetings of the SUS were attracting more than 50 people. On July 4, 1993, *The Washington Post* did an article about the SUS. Shortly after, we started receiving calls from people outside the World Bank who wanted to attend. After one year, SUS was attracting 50 to 80 people every week. Subsidiary groups were set up on other days of the week to discuss specific topics such as mind/body healing and *A Course in Miracles*. A meditation group also started. I tell this story to illustrate two points—first, the importance of open communications with your soul; and, second, the great thirst that exists for the expression of spiritual values in the workplace.

Embracing your soul

Listening to your soul is the first step toward openly communicating with higher dimensions of consciousness. Beyond listening lies embracing. Learning to *embrace* your soul requires you to adopt principles and values that exist in the timeless, unified energy field of the higher dimensions of consciousness. This world knows no boundaries, no fear, and no duality and recognizes only unconditional love. The soul remains the eternal aspect of your being that has known many lives. While not necessary to believe in reincarnation to explore your soul, getting in touch with your soul's other lives can bring understanding to aspects of your present life circumstances.

This journey we call life, with its unfathomable beginning and its inexplicable end, is just one of hundreds of lives that your soul has led. Every living experience has been important to the soul. None more important than another, each one focused on learning some aspect of unconditional love. We, as three-dimensional beings, see only part of this process in which we are involved. We see only our present life. We have no immediate recall of the other lives of our soul. We have no idea why we are the way we are in this lifetime. But for the soul it is very clear. Your present life is the next step in your soul's journey. If you understand this, you will also understand that the circumstances of this lifetime are part of the natural flow of an experiential learning system designed by your soul to promote its own evolution.

The circumstances of your life are part of the natural flow of an experiential learning system designed by your soul to promote its own evolution.

As humans, with our limited one-life perspective, we find this very difficult to comprehend. Deep down we know in some way we are involved in a learning process. We call it spiritual growth. This is a misnomer. In reality, this process is more like unfoldment. As souls we have forgotten our oneness with all creation, become totally absorbed in our earthly experiences, and forgotten who we are. As humans we are trying to help our souls recall the perfection that was ours at the time of creation. All the lessons the soul designs for us focus on this singular purpose. The layers of belief systems that we have created in our minds separate us from our true being. These layers of beliefs are like the petals that form the bud of a flower. Just as the full beauty of the flower cannot be seen until the petals unfold, we cannot rediscover our perfection until we peel away the layers of beliefs which surround us. When we become like an open flower, we have no nooks and crannies to hide our shadow-self. Everything is seen. Nothing is hidden. The beauty of our soul is visible for the world to behold.

The real journey of life is one of inner discovery. Understanding your soul nature brings a new perspective to your life—a perspective that takes away the fear of death, and the fear of living. This understanding empowers you to create the reality you want, and fills every moment of your life with meaning. The feeling of being alive becomes the most exciting thing in your life. Everything in our external world represents our individual and collective state of consciousness. We have no need to search in dusty libraries to find out about ourselves and our society. What happens in our lives every moment completely reflects the state of our personal and communal inner being. We simply need to observe.

Accelerating your unfoldment

The most important service we can render to our soul is to accelerate its unfoldment. We must give it a free reign to express itself through our personality. This process involves personal transformation through the personality's attunement with the soul. As you progress with your attunement, you become a channel for the expression of unconditional love. The process involves four changes in awareness. First, *recognize yourself as a being of multidimensional consciousness—accept the fact that you are a soul living in the third dimension of consciousness.* When you fully accept this as your reality, you have made the decision to accelerate the process of soul evolution.

Second, *acknowledge soul and ego responsibility for creating your personal reality, and the contribution you make to creating the global reality.* The principle of responsibility must be fully accepted. Your world is *your* creation of reality and my world is *my* creation of reality. We may experience exactly the same life event, but we give it different meanings. The meaning we give to it individually will be based on personal belief systems closely linked to each individual soul's state of evolution. This concept may be difficult to accept. I know how long I struggled with it. The victim approach is very seductive.

Whatever energy you put out into the world is the energy that you attract. Look carefully at your life circumstances and if you do not like what you see, make a change in the direction of unconditional love. Watch for the positive changes that will certainly occur.

Third, *look constantly for your fear-based beliefs*. When you find them, understand them, own them, and release them. Their energy prevents you from living in unconditional love. These beliefs are not difficult to discover. Whenever you feel emotional discomfort, you are dealing with a fear-based belief. Your "negative" experiences do not happen by chance. You either attract them through the energy you put out into the world, or create them through the meaning you give to your experiences. In certain cases they may represent an intervention of the soul. Whatever the case, regard all discomforting events as positive signposts that demand a change of belief.

Finally, *recognize that spiritual unfoldment involves interacting in the world*. There is no more perfect laboratory for learning the true expression of your soul than through the fullness of life's experiences and relationships. When we avoid relationships, we avoid practical applications of what we learn. We cannot unfold if we have no mirror to reflect back to us the progress we are making. Relationships function as temples of learning.

When you make the decision to live as a soul, you will need a new road map, a new way of understanding the world, and a new belief system. Base your new belief system on the principles that govern the higher realms of consciousness. Replace your beliefs about time, space, and materiality with new beliefs that embrace the concepts of eternity, omnipresence, and energy. As you integrate these new concepts into your life, your beliefs will change. You will move out of the comfort zone of society's belief systems into a realm where you stand out as someone different. This, in itself, will create new fears. You will feel exposed, unsure of yourself, afraid to speak out. These fears are your passport to transformation. As you walk into them and through them, you will experience your unfoldment. As you emerge, you will feel empowered and alive. More closely attuned with your soul, you will be living in soul consciousness.

If it sometimes happens that your own hand inadvertently strikes you, would you take a stick and chastise your hand for its heedfulness, and thus add to your pain? It is the same when your neighbor, whose soul is one with yours, because of insufficient understanding, does you harm: should you retaliate, it would be you who would suffer. Rabbi Shmelke of Nikolsburg

We must raise prodigiously the threshold of our awareness so that we could see ourselves for what we really are: individual cells in the immortal body of humanity. Norman Cousins

It is not the level of prosperity that makes for happiness but the kinship of heart to heart and the way we look at the world. Both are attitudes within our power, so that a man is happy so long as he chooses to be happy, and no one can stop him.
Alexander Solzhenitsyn

The two are really only one: it is only the ignorant person who sees many when there is only one. Black Elk

10

Five Pathways to Unity

There is only one fundamental principle—unity—that we need to integrate into our lives to achieve soul consciousness. By integrating values that support unity in our daily living, we grow closer to our souls. As we connect with the oneness that exists in the higher levels of consciousness, we develop a new way of "seeing" and "knowing." Our psychic powers develop and we learn to listen closely to our inner voice—to the voice of our soul.

Synchronicity

One of the first ways we begin to notice the connection that exists at the higher levels of consciousness is through serendipity and synchronicity. In 1754, Horace Walpole coined the word "serendipity" to describe the faculty of making fortunate discoveries by accident. Very often, with the wisdom of hindsight, such "accidents" take on new meaning. They form part of a pattern of experiences that lead us in a certain direction, as if we are being guided by a hidden hand. In my own life, such events occur frequently. When I am ready for the next step in my unfoldment, I meet someone, find a book, or experience an event that perfectly matches my needs, even if do not consciously know those needs. On many occasions I have gone to a book store, not knowing exactly what I was looking for, and immediately found a book that provided an insight that took me another step into my journey of unfoldment. In recent years, I have "accidently" met or been put in contact with a constant stream of people who have had a significant impact on my life and my work. Viewed from a higher perspective, these formed a completely rational pattern of experiences. Viewed from a three-dimensional perspective, they were simply accidents of chance.

The concept of serendipity was expanded by Carl Jung in his definition of synchronicity.[1] He defined synchronicity as "the coincidence in time of two or more causally unrelated events which have the same meaning." Thinking about a close friend and receiving a call from that person a few moments later would be an example of synchronicity. The thought and the telephone call are the unrelated events; the common meaning is that they both concern the friend.

The concept of synchronicity arose from the merger of quantum theory and psychology. This merger occurred through collaboration between Carl Jung and Wolfgang Pauli. Although the origin of quantum mechanics is credited to Werner Heisenberg, his friend Pauli deserved the credit for convincing many physicists that quantum mechanics was correct. Jung was influenced and encouraged by Pauli to publish his ideas on synchronicity. The Jung-Pauli collaboration resulted in the publication of *The Interpretation and Nature of the Psyche.*[2] Through their interactions, the concept of "meaning" entered into the idea of synchronicity. Through synchronicity, exterior manifestations mirror interior transformations of the mind. Recognizing the relationships between exterior manifestations and internal changes endow meaning to these exterior manifestations that at first seem unrelated to any other events. Jung describes the following circumstance as an example of synchronicity.

My example concerns a young woman patient who, in spite of efforts made on both sides, proved to be psychologically inaccessible. The difficulty lay in the fact that she always knew better about everything. Her excellent education had provided her with a weapon ideally suited to this purpose, namely a highly polished Cartesian rationalism with an impeccably "geometrical" idea of reality. After several fruitless attempts to sweeten her rationalism with a somewhat more human understanding I had to confine myself to the hope that something unexpected and irrational would turn up, something that would burst the intellectual retort into which she had sealed herself. I was sitting opposite her one day, with my back to the window, listening to her flow of rhetoric. She had an impressive dream the night before, in which someone had given her a golden scarab—a costly piece of jewelry. While she was still telling me this dream, I heard something behind me gently tapping on the window. I turned round and saw that it was a fairly large flying insect that was knocking against the windowpane from the outside in the obvious effort to get into the dark room. This seemed to me very strange. I opened the window immediately and caught the insect in the air as it flew in. It was a scarabeid beetle, or common rose-chafer, whose gold-green color most nearly resembles that of a golden scarab. I handed the beetle to my patient with the words, "Here is your scarab." This experience punctured the desired hole in her rationalism and broke the ice of her intellectual resistance. The treatment could now be continued with satisfactory results.[3]

The separate events of the dream and the appearance of the beetle completely contrast with our normal experiences of cause and effect. Our normal experiences of cause and effect are physically obvious—like when billiard balls rebound off one another. The difference with synchronistic events is that they bridge the gap between mind and matter and occur without regard to space and time. In *Synchronicity: The bridge between matter and mind,* David Peat notes:

> Pauli believed that synchronicity made it possible to begin a dialogue between physics and psychology in such a way that the subjective would be introduced into physics and the objective into psychology. Rather than looking exclusively to physics or psychology alone for the solution to nature's secrets, Pauli felt that a complementary approach was called for in which subjective and objective aspects would reveal different features of the same underlying phenomena.[4]

Jung initially identified synchronicities as the outer world's reflections of inner changes in consciousness. He later went on to define three categories of synchronistic events: the coincidence of an external event with a dream or thought where there is no evidence of any connection (synchronicity); the coincidence of an external event outside the field of perception with knowledge of that event (simultaneous knowledge); and the coincidence of inner knowing about an event that takes place in the future (prior knowledge). From his studies, Jung concluded that either the psyche (soul) cannot be localized in space or time, or space and time are relative to the psyche.[5] In other words, he affirms the spaceless and timeless nature of soul consciousness. When you begin to pay attention to the voice of your soul, you will notice all three categories of synchronicity occurring in your life. Increasing awareness of these phenomena in my own life has led me to conclude that there are no chance events. All events are meaningful and are totally connected at some level of the mind. We are connected in consciousness to all there is. When we truly believe this, we affirm the existence of unity consciousness.

Unity

We implement the principle of unity by overcoming our beliefs in separation. In the higher realms of consciousness, we all form part of a vast flux of energy. According to physicist David Bohm, everything is enfolded into everything.[5] We are separate only to the extent that a wave is separate in an ocean. The wave has a distinct and separate form, but eventually it folds back into the ocean and the water that formed the first wave forms another wave. We can only achieve an awareness of the unity and connectedness of everything by undoing the sense of fragmentation in our minds. We need to reidentify and re-integrate ourselves into this unity. Returning to the example above, we are like waves that believe they are separate from the ocean.

We can help our souls attain unity consciousness by embracing beliefs consistent with the values and principles of unity. There are many beliefs that reflect the principle of unity consciousness. I believe the following five are the most important. When we adopt these beliefs—respect for all life, equality of all souls, importance of the common good, responsibility for the whole, and unconditional love—they become pathways to unity consciousness. We must incorporate these principles in our relationships with self, family, colleagues, friends, flora and fauna, our environment, and planet Earth.

Responsibility for the whole

When you recognize that you are part of the unity of all things you then become very aware of the impact your life has on others and the environment. Until this recognition dawns, as long as you are happy you will not care too much about how you affect others. When you accept the principle of unity, your joy will become the happiness of others.

We achieve unity by expanding our self-identity. Whatever you identify with you care for. When you identify with your body, you care for it. When you identify with members of your

> *Whatever you identify with you care for.*

family, you support them. When you identify with your home and garden, you care for them. When you identify with your environment, you protect and nurture it. As you expand your sense of identity, you also expand the range of your caring. To reach unity consciousness, the caring must attain the quality of unconditional love for all creation. You must lose yourself in the oneness. The wave must become the ocean. This is the primary task of our souls.

When I realized the importance of bringing unity into my life, I gave up my past identity and began to consider myself as a citizen of the world, and a member of all races and religious faiths. I began to consider my principal identity to be a soul having a human experience. Although in this life I am expressing my soul energy in the physical form as a male, I possess considerable feminine energy that I feel free to express. This identity I have chosen allows me to be inclusive in all my relationships and to live outside separation. If I had not consciously made this choice, I would have continued to think of myself as a Yorkshire man and Protestant. In so doing, I would have felt a sense of separation from the rest of the British people and Europeans, and I would have felt separate from Catholics, Jews, and Muslims. As a soul, I am free to connect with all these people because in soul consciousness there are no geographical boundaries and no distinctions. Thus, by focusing on what we all share, I eliminate the boundaries of separation that could keep us apart. All wars throughout history have been fought between groups with different identities to protect or expand their national boundaries, religions, or races. People who share the same identity rarely declare war on each other.

As you approach unity consciousness, your sense of self expands. This larger sense of self gives you a greater sense of responsibility. Because you now identify with humanity, the earth, and nature, you care for them. Their welfare becomes closely linked to your own. You feel the need to defend them and nurture them. In this state you are intensely aware of the external impact of your life on other people and your surroundings. You are concerned that your actions do not harm others, or pollute the environment, and you do as much as you can to care for those who are disadvantaged, underprivileged, or sick. As you lose yourself in the service of humanity, you lessen the focus on your own needs. You concentrate less on getting what you think you need and much more on giving. The movement of your energy is outward, toward others, rather than inwards towards yourself.

Importance of the common good

We recognize the importance of the common good through acts of sharing and cooperation. Apart from basic needs—food, water, and shelter—our physical needs are few. After we have met those needs, we focus our desires on things that will increase convenience and comfort in our lives. When we have reached a certain degree of comfort, theoretically we should not have any other needs. In reality, fueled by our fears and insecurities and our constant search for pleasure, we continue creating more needs. We keep on spending and accumulating. At this level we seek only to fill our inner emptiness. The emptiness we feel reflects the fact that we have forgotten who we are, and measures our disconnection from soul and unity consciousness. We seek to fill this internal emptiness through amassing external wealth or physical objects. The effect is always temporary. We fail to understand that objects we possess become part of our identity. Whatever we care for becomes a part of whom we are.

If your identity is wrapped up in your possessions or your bank account, then your possessions and your bank account will dominate your thinking. You will be forever worrying about how to protect them. When you embrace unity consciousness, you see your possessions differently. They become impediments to finding your true self. This is not to say that it is necessary to give away all your possessions to find unity consciousness. You must simply be aware of the temporary nature of your custodianship and act accordingly. In reality, you own nothing. There is nothing separate to own. As a steward or temporary guardian of your possessions and wealth, the question you should be asking yourself is, how can I use what I have for the common good?

Sharing and cooperation will very often be the response to that question. Contributing your talents and resources and cooperating with others make it possible to achieve synergies where the results are more than the sum of the parts. Cooperation fully reflects the principle of unity consciousness. It brings people together, builds relationships, conserves resources, shares benefits, creates equality, and shows that you care about others. Cooperation fosters "win-win" solutions that promote the common good. Competition, on the other hand, promotes separation. It creates winners and losers and haves and have-nots, destroys relationships, wastes resources, promotes selfish interest, and seeks supremacy.

There can be unity only when people are free. Unity is a choice and cannot be imposed.

Equality of all souls

We recognize the equality of all souls through freedom of expression and equal rights. Without freedom we cannot express ourselves fully and we cannot learn responsibility. This principle is fully understood in the higher dimensions of consciousness. There can be unity only when people are free. Unity is a choice and cannot be imposed. It behooves each one of us and society at large to ensure that we allow every soul manifesting in the physical plane of consciousness the freedom of choice. This is a precondition for spiritual unfoldment.

At the soul level we are all equal. When we adopt a superior attitude toward another, or consider ourselves to be better than others, we simply cover up our own feelings of inadequacy. We put others down to feel good about ourselves. The deprecating judgments we make about others represent aspects of our shadow projecting themselves into the outer world. When this happens, we are operating in the realm of three-dimensional consciousness. Our own fears of inferiority cause us to behave this way. When we accept ourselves as we really are and release our fears of inadequacy, we find it easy to accept others as they really are.

The implementation of the belief in equality begins in your own home with your children and spouse. Equality demands an open and honest atmosphere where there is no fear. The greatest gift we can give another person is freedom from fear. The most we can do in this respect is provide the conditions that nurture loving, honest, and open relationships. We cannot take away people's fears. Only they can do that.

At a global level, equality of people has reigned as one of the most contentious issues of the 20th century. Beginning with women and their freedom to vote, it moved on to embrace racial issues, and the rights of minorities. Although progress has been made on all these fronts, there remain sizeable unfinished agendas that still need to be addressed. The major issue of equality we face in the next century is overcoming poverty—reducing the growing gap between the haves and have-nots.

Current economic belief systems are constructed and operated in such a manner that the rich get richer and the poor get poorer. This applies both within nations and between nations and is intimately linked to the global environmental crisis. Both the overconsumption by the rich industrialized countries and the poverty of developing nations fuel the environmental degradation of the planet. The engines that drive the world's economy force people away from sustainable lifestyles on the land and create urban ghettos. Until our political systems and trade agreements recognize the importance of sharing wealth and resources in environmentally friendly ways among all peoples equitably, we will continue on the present path of despair.

Respect for all life

We respect life through caring and protecting all living things. Every form of life is a manifestation of soul consciousness. They, too, are using their experiences in the physical plane of consciousness to learn lessons. They have a right to live out their soul purpose just as we do. We should learn to accommodate the needs of all creation in the environment in which we live. As we understand this concept, we begin to act as stewards. We begin to recognize that we are accountable to all soul energies. As humans we have the ability to destroy or preserve our natural environment. We have the freedom and the responsibility to choose whether to allow other soul energies to live out their lives in our world. Our record so far has not been good. We have allowed numerous species of plants and animals to become extinct. As we learn respect for life, we build our connection to other aspects of soul consciousness. By destroying our natural world, we exhibit a belief in separation.

As we come to recognize ourselves as souls, we overcome the fear of death and begin to understand the eternal nature of our awareness. Eternal life is a self-evident fact in the fourth dimension of consciousness. This understanding has major implications for our three-dimensional belief systems, as it takes us out of the short-term view of life into the long-term view. As reincarnating souls, we are the future generations. We are creating our heritage at this very moment. The conditions that we will experience on the earth in our future incarnations are the conditions that we are now creating. If you do not embrace the concept of reincarnation, then simply think about the impact that your present decisions will have on your children and future generations. Do you want to leave the planet in a better or worse condition for them? The earth is our connection to future generations. The quality of their inheritance depends on what we leave behind. If we feel connected to them, then we will leave behind something better than what we found. If we feel separate, we will not care. We will exploit everything for our own selfish interests. By choosing to care about future generations and the diverse manifestations of soul consciousness that abound on the earth, we embrace unity consciousness.

Unconditional love

Through service we express our recognition of unconditional love. When unity is recognized, giving becomes the same as receiving. If we are all cells in the same body, then we can give only to ourselves. When the strong cells of a body give to the weak cells, the strength of the whole body increases. We must care for the weak, the disabled, and minorities to increase the strength of the whole. It is in everyone's interest to do so. This strategy fully reflects the principle of unity.

Joy will elude us however, if our service to others is not based on unconditional giving. When service is given with the expectation of return, it becomes conditional and ceases to be a pathway to joy. When you feel needy of love, your secret hope is that by giving love you will get love in return. This strategy is rarely successful and always results in pain and separation. The basis of such a belief is the fear that you are not loved. You attract whatever you fear. As discussed earlier, this is one of the principal operating rules of consciousness.

In a relationship where both persons are in touch with their souls, they are full of love. There is no emptiness inside. Each person focuses on *giving* love

When unity is recognized, giving becomes the same as receiving.

away, not attracting love. With this unconditional giving, no demands are felt; there are no hidden agendas in the relationship. Communication can now be honest and truthful. In this type of relationship there is nothing to fear. The more love you give, the more you receive. In consciousness terms everything is energy. The more positive, loving, unconditional energy you put out into the world, be it in the form of caring, money, or a positive attitude, the more you get back. Giving service is the fastest track there is to bliss. What better incentive could we have for embracing unity consciousness.

Progress toward unity consciousness can be hastened by focusing on five goals: importance of the common good, equality of all souls, responsibility for the whole, respect for all life, and unconditional love. As you learn to fully integrate these beliefs into your life and adopt the values they represent, you find yourself forming a more meaningful relationship with the world around you. The process accelerates as you consciously embrace your soul. You will find yourself totally supported by unseen forces that provide for your needs in a timely manner.

Expect the best: convert problems into opportunities; be dissatisfied with the status quo; focus on where you want to go, instead of where you're coming from; and most importantly, decide to be happy, knowing it's an attitude, a habit gained from daily practice, and not as a result or payoff. Dennis Waitley

Men are disturbed not by things, but by the view they take of them. Epictetus

To know the truth one must get rid of knowledge; nothing is more powerful and creative than emptiness. Lao Tse

There is no need to struggle to be free; the absence of struggle is in itself freedom. Chogyam Trungpa

The only way to discover the limits of the possible is to go beyond them to the impossible. Arthur C. Clarke

Peace of mind comes not from wanting to change others, but, by simply accepting them as they are. Gerald Jampolsky

11

Ten Strategies for Attaining Soul Consciousness

The five pathways to unity discussed in the preceding chapter are beliefs that we need to integrate into our lives if we wish to live in alignment with our soul. They provide a large-scale map of the soul's journey. Such a map is important, but not sufficient. When we explore new territory, we also need information about what strategies to adopt in case we get lost. Below you will find such information. The ten strategies for achieving soul consciousness provide guidance for those seeking to live in alignment with their soul.

Strategy 1: Beliefs condition your reality

When you accept the challenge to "know yourself," you embark on a journey that leads to the soul's recovery. Self-knowledge begins with questioning your every thought, word, and action. Why do I think that? Why did I do that? Why did I say that? Posing such questions will help you uncover your hidden motives and beliefs. When you begin to consider your responses, you will be surprised by the fears and assumptions you unearth. Your fears and assumptions act as belief filters through which you sieve reality. What you see and hear is what you have programmed yourself to see and hear. The coping responses that helped you survive childhood and the ideas about yourself that you gleaned from your parents, siblings, and peers, crystallized over time into beliefs through which you now filter reality. You unconsciously translate your experiences into the mold of your beliefs. Whatever these beliefs are, they act as sieves through which you condition your reality. With these unconscious filters in place, your life becomes a self-imposed illusion. Your pathway to self discovery lies in removing these filters so that you may encounter truth.

The following story illustrates my point. A young man named Roger was in his early twenties. One of Roger's greatest thrills was to take his sports car into the mountains near his home and drive as fast as he could around tight corners. This pursuit reinforced Roger's masculine image of himself. One day, as he was driving alone in the mountains and approaching one of his favorite series of bends with a precipice on one side and a meadow on the other, a car shot around the bend in front of him and swerved from one side to the other. The car was out of control and heading straight for him. He knew it was too late to avoid a crash unless something miraculous happened. At the last moment, the driver of the other car regained control and pulled over to the other side of the road, missing Roger's car by inches. As the cars sped past each other, the female driver in the other car turned toward Roger and yelled, "Pig!" Without thinking, Roger instinctively yelled back, "Cow!" His immediate thought afterwards was that he had done well to respond quickly to this woman's aggression. Roger managed to regain his composure and swept around the bend a little faster than he would have liked. As he came out of the bend, he found a pig in the middle of the road. Fortunately, he managed to stop in time.

Roger's belief system filtered the woman's "Pig" comment as aggression. To be put in fear of his life by a female was a blow to his self-esteem. He was angry at her for making him feel that way. Roger filtered her message as aggression and retaliated accordingly. Meanwhile, the woman who sent a message of warning based on love interpreted his "Cow" response as concern for her safety. She was now anticipating finding a cow in the road. Roger used a "fear" filter, and she used a "love" filter. Neither of the two drivers received the intended message. They both filtered events based on their beliefs, neither of which represented the truth. This story is frequently enacted by all of us in one form or another, throughout our lives. We all constantly filter life's events through our belief systems.

Strategy 2: Practice self-observation

If we could actually achieve transcendence—live in a world without beliefs—what would that experience feel like? We would be completely immersed in just being. We would have no fears to drag us into the future and no anger to pull us into the past. Our awareness would be fully focused in the present moment and we would feel a profound state of joy and peace. We would have no fear beliefs to separate us from those we came into contact with, or from our environment. We would see all life, including our own, from the position of a detached observer. In this higher state we would be open to truth, free to choose when to act and when to speak, rather than respond from the unconscious. We would not need to defend ourselves in any way or in any situation since we would be without fear. Our relationships would be open to cooperation, goodwill, and sharing. We would become perfect listeners. We would be completely open to the wisdom and intuition that flow from the soul.

One of the ways we enter the no-belief state and grow in self-knowledge is through self-observation. The observer that is in you is the projection of your soul. It is the "I" at the center of your being. It is the "I" you become in meditation when your mind is unclouded by thought. Finding the "I" that is the observer means giving up your fears and the beliefs about whom you think you are. How we identify ourselves conditions our thoughts, words, and actions. The identities we assume are beliefs about whom we are. When we give up the beliefs that create our identity, we find our true selves. Only when we move our awareness to the soul-self can we be truly an observer.

Whenever you feel any form of emotional discomfort—anger, frustration, or resentment—seek out that part of your identity that is feeling these things and attempt to discover why. You will learn much about your ego from questioning yourself. However, to do this exercise you must detach from the part of you that is having these feelings. Learning to become an observer is essential if you want to remove yourself from the grip of your unconscious conditioning. The more you identify with your soul the easier this becomes.

Strategy 3: Every event is neutral

One important way of removing the biases of your belief system is to consider every event to be neutral. By affirming that all events are neutral, you recognize that whatever you feel about the situation comes from the meaning you choose to give it. However, it may not be a conscious choice. If an event brings up negative feelings and anger, you can be sure that you are dealing with unconscious fear beliefs. The real issue is not with the external situation, but with your own lack of attunement with your soul. Whenever you encounter emotional discomfort or anger, it is always about yourself; it is never about others.

By affirming that all events are neutral, you are giving yourself the space to observe yourself and examine the belief filter that is causing distress. As you learn to do this, you will identify situations that consistently bring about negative reactions. This identification will serve as an important clue to determining the belief filters that cause you discomfort. Talk to yourself as if you were an observer. Say things like, "Now (insert your name), what is going on here? Why are you getting angry? Come on, do not play the victim with me, tell me the real reason. What is the fear that you are not admitting to?" When you can consistently attain this level of detachment, you are on the path to recovery. When you realize that your reactions are based on your choices, then you can begin to work on changing your beliefs.

By rigorously applying this technique, your unconscious beliefs will become apparent. You will begin to see a pattern in the way you interpret events. You will begin to unearth your hidden fears. Over time, you will gradually be able to master your beliefs and your emotions. You will find that the instantaneous panic that was once triggered by certain events is now controllable.

Strategy 4: Every problem is an opportunity

The situations we encounter in life become problems only if the actions we believe are necessary to resolve them cause us fear. Fear is the only difference between a problem and an opportunity. When you live in soul consciousness there is no fear and every problem is an opportunity. However, the opportunity always requires us to express the values associated with unity consciousness. As soon as you classify a situation as a problem, then you should move into the self-observation mode and tell yourself that you are giving the situation all the meaning it has for you. When you have done that, try to see what opportunities the situation can provide. Is it an opportunity for cooperation rather than competition? Is it an opportunity for expressing unconditional love? Is it an opportunity for being honest and truthful about your relationship? Is it an opportunity to open your heart? What is the opportunity the situation is providing?

Learning to interpret what is happening, without critical judgment or having your emotions cloud your thinking, is the first step in seeing events as opportunities. If

Problems are opportunities underpinned by fear.

you cannot stop the emotional response, take a few moments to experience it and let it go. Then move into acceptance. You may be creating the meaning of the situation through your beliefs, or you may be attracting the situation because of the energy you are putting out into the world. It may even be your soul intervening in your life to get your attention. The only thing you can be sure about is that, whatever is happening, there is a message in it for you. You are never a victim. Your ego and your soul always create your reality for a good reason. Behind every painful event there is a force for good. It may not seem like that when it happens, but you can be sure the good is there. Pain and suffering are our friends. They are signposts directing us to think about situations differently. When we seize the opportunity and make permanent changes, we see positive results. When we feel victimized, we allow another opportunity to go by and set ourselves up for a repeat of the same sad lesson.

Beware of rationalizing what is going on in your life. It is time and energy consuming and a waste of both resources. With your limited three-dimensional perspective and the belief system you inherited from the past, your chances of stumbling on the truth of a particular situation are slim.

The logic we use while living in three-dimensional consciousness takes no account of our unconscious beliefs, or of the soul perspective. Our understanding of a situation often has more to do with our beliefs than with the truth. If you want to know the truth, turn inwards and engage in a dialogue with your soul. Seek your answers in meditation by asking and active listening. This is not as difficult as it sounds. Your soul is ready to speak with you and advise you at any time you wish. Ask and it will be given. Seek and you shall find. Ask for guidance just before going to sleep, and pay attention to your dreams. Do not expect to hear voices. Your soul is more likely to communicate with you through visions, images, and thoughts. Pay particular attention to your early morning thoughts, especially when you have asked for help the night before.

> *Our understanding of a situation often has more to do with our beliefs than with the truth.*

Strategy 5: Trust in a supporting universe

When you fear the world you live in, you will find it unsupportive. When you love the world you live in, you will find continual support. Your belief creates your reality. Those who believe in a hostile universe want to control all aspects of their lives, particularly their relationships. Very often they will suffer from allergies. Allergies are symptomatic of a belief in a hostile world. Whatever we unconsciously fear we attract. The process of unfoldment requires that we release our fears and give control of our lives to our soul. When you do this, you open yourself to the support from the universe.

As you progress with your unfoldment, you may be presented with opportunities that do not fit your idea of how things should evolve. You may also encounter what you believe are setbacks. It is important that you do not prejudge or constrain the way in which the universe works, and remember—all problems are opportunities in disguise. Sometimes it takes tremendous pain and discomfort to make us realize that we need to change. What can appear to be a major setback, such as a divorce, losing your job, or a loved one, is nothing less than an opening to a new future that would never have arisen if the "setback" had not occurred.

The universe is a totally supporting environment for your soul. The physical realm was created by souls for souls—how could it be other than supportive? If you feel the universe is not supporting you, either you have not yet accepted yourself as a soul, or you have not accepted the lessons that your soul chose for you in this lifetime.

Once you have committed yourself to spiritual unfoldment and the recovery of your soul, the events that befall you will lead you to your soul's desire. It is important to trust in the process and allow your life to unfold without judgment. Later, as you look back, you

The soul never gives you a task that you are not equipped to handle.

will see how perfectly the unfoldment took place. You will see how you were given what was necessary at the moment it was necessary, and how your openness to change accelerated the process. Integrating your personality with your soul gives control of your life to a higher force. It is essential during this process to substitute the agenda of your ego for that of your soul. If you still seek status through your career promotions or wealth, or through the manipulation of others, then your unfoldment will be blocked. When your personality truly reflects your soul's purpose, you exchange your career for a mission. You become a server of humanity, forming part of a global network of world servers, seeking to move humanity and the planet into a new age of enlightenment.

When you pay attention to your soul purpose, you will find that the work you are called to do always helps you to develop and grow. The soul never gives you a task that you are not equipped to handle. It may feel as if you are taking on something for which your skills are inadequate. However, you will find that the help you need will always be there at exactly the right moment. After many years of doubting myself, I learned how to deal with the fear of inadequacy. Let me illustrate my technique.

One day my boss called me into his office and told me there was a new project that he wanted me to handle. I asked him if it was a difficult project. He answered that it was. I told him that I was not interested because I only wanted to work on impossible projects. So he assigned me an impossible project and I completed it. Why do I like demanding, seemingly impossible tasks? The answer is simple. If the task seems impossible, then you are forced to rely on your soul and its linkages to higher realms of consciousness to get the job done. You have no alternative, unless you want to live in anxiety and fear. When you enlist the universe of consciousness and all its connections, you move from fear to trust. You become a channel for higher powers to help you create a solution. You move into a state of connectedness that attracts synchronistic experiences.

When you recognize the connectivity of consciousness, you understand the normal operation of consciousness at the soul level. The soul is able to contact and exchange information with other souls without your being aware of it. By committing to the impossible, you have no alternative but to embrace your soul. You say no to fear and yes to the unity of the universe.

Strategy 6: Value yourself

If you do not value yourself, nobody else will. Your outer experience will always reflect your inner consciousness. If you cannot love yourself, then you will have difficulty maintaining loving relationships with others. The more we love ourselves the more others will love us. Loving yourself is not a selfish act. It is a recognition of the importance that you attach to contributing to the strength of the whole. Acts of love toward yourself can take many forms. The most important are making sure that you have time for yourself and your pursuits and saying "no" to situations which demand more than you can give. If you always serve others' needs and deny yourself, you may be living in fear of not being loved. Self-denial is very often a strategy for getting love from others.

In many situations, particularly when you are under stress, saying no is the most appropriate and loving thing you can do. When you say yes but mean no, your personality is out of alignment with your soul. You are letting fear dictate your reaction. When you are unable to cope, say so. This helps everyone. If you are working for someone, letting them know that you are having difficulty helps that person have a realistic expectation of when the job might be finished. If you give an expectation that is not realistic, then disappointment follows the deception. Being honest toward yourself, and to others, is the most loving thing you can do. It is a basic skill that we should all learn.

If we have fear in our hearts, we are unable to be honest with ourselves and others. Fear either prevents us from speaking up or forces us to lie. Remember that fear is the memory of past pain projected into the future. Behind the fear is a belief that speaking up or being honest will result in punishment. These beliefs often have their origin in childhood when we learned that speaking our thoughts, or expressing our emotions, was not always appreciated by our parents or teachers. We learned that speaking up could result in suffering. The pain of this memory often prevents us from speaking up.

When our fear beliefs prevent us from saying what we feel, we block the outward flow of thought energy and store it in our emotions (an emotion is an unexpressed thought). We feel frustrated and angry (a feeling of not being cared for) but are afraid to release our unexpressed thoughts because of the imagined consequences. As a result, we keep quiet and adapt to living in fear. Our mind becomes a pressure cooker of unexpressed thoughts and our blood pressure rises. We believe that there is nothing we can do about the situation.

Some people release the pressure by projecting their anger onto an unsuspecting world. Since they are afraid to express their feelings to the one with whom they are angry, they project it onto a subordinate or anyone who crosses their path. Eventually, the negative energy will express itself. It either takes the form of sickness or an emotional outburst. This may be the stored up energy of a lifetime or it may be the energy of the previous day. If we have blocked energy long enough, we could eventually let it out in a wild rampage. Loving yourself begins when you give yourself permission to freely express your thoughts and take care of your own needs.

How we feel about ourselves governs our reality. When we are high on self-esteem, we attract positive and loving situations. When we are low on self-esteem, we attract negative situations and fearful thoughts. In *The Six Pillars of Self Esteem*, Nathaniel Branden provides six strategies for building self-esteem: living consciously, self-acceptance, self-responsibility, self-assertiveness, living purpose-fully, and personal integrity.[1]

When you **live consciously,** you give up imagining that your feelings are an infallible guide to truth. You recognize that your feelings reflect your beliefs. Your beliefs are based on subjective experiences that may not coincide with reality.

When you accept yourself fully, you own the negative and positive aspects of your persona. Without **self-acceptance**, you deny those parts of your consciousness that you dislike about yourself and only see them in others.

Self-responsibility affirms your role in creating your reality. You are responsible for your own happiness. No one else can give it to you or take it away from you.

Self-assertiveness allows you to treat yourself with respect in all human encounters. By asking questions and saying no, you give yourself the right to exist and participate in the world in a constructive way.

Living purposefully gives meaning to your life. Without a purpose you will drift from one expediency to another, accomplishing very little and having little sense of achievement. Living purposefully means consciously deciding what it is you want to do with your life and doing it. There can be no greater purpose and meaning in life than to be fully engaged in your soul's purpose.

Personal integrity involves living your life according to your personal ethic. When your thoughts, words, and actions coincide with your beliefs, then you have integrity. However, if your personal ethic does not coincide with the values of unity consciousness, you will find pain, discomfort, and suffering occurring in your life, even though you may be living in integrity. The ultimate ethic is spiritually based and reflects the values of unity consciousness.

Selfworth. The most common self-esteem issue is low selfworth. When you have low selfworth, you imagine yourself as unlovable, unlikable, not good enough, not smart enough or incapable. Reality for you is a constant denial of self. You will be unsuccessful in whatever areas your negation of self manifests. As you tackle your issues, you will be working with affirmations that support positive feelings about yourself, that affirm you as a capable person and worthy of love.

Jane's story illustrates many of these points. Jane, an attractive woman in her late 30's, had become extremely depressed after she broke up a four-year relationship with John. All she wanted was to be with John, and every night she cried herself to sleep.

Jane's belief was that she was unlovable. This was one of her life's metaphors. She had been one of five children and grew up competing for the attention of her parents. But her parents had their own problems. Her father was an alcoholic and her mother lived in fear of her father. The children always seemed to be in the way. Jane never felt validated as a person in her childhood. Jane's experiences reinforced her belief that she was unlovable. Moreover, she never experienced unconditional love. As an adult her belief became a filter that conditioned her experiences and reflected in her relationships with men. No matter how hard her partners tried to show their love for her, for Jane it was never totally believable. She lived in a state of anxiety about her appearance and her ability to attract and hold her partner's affection. What she feared became her reality. John, like the other men before him, could never fill the emptiness that Jane felt inside. In the end, they tired of being mistrusted and misunderstood and left Jane.

As Jane realized this and accepted responsibility for the belief that was creating her reality, she knew she must release the pain of her childhood experiences if she were to overcome her disabling belief. She sought counseling and, little by little, she was able to build her confidence. She began to see herself as desirable and independent. It took much patience and hard work on Jane's part to release her limiting beliefs and replace them with positive beliefs. Now she is happily married and no longer feels the need for validation that she frequently felt in the past.

Strategy 7: Acceptance

Acceptance of the conditions your soul has chosen for you in this lifetime is essential if you wish to live in soul consciousness. Equally important is acceptance of the need for change. Spiritual unfoldment is an evolutionary process that hinges on change. Acceptance of conditions and the need for change involves three stages—gratitude, surrender, and joy. Expressing gratitude to the soul (or to God) for your life creates a connection to the higher dimensions of consciousness. Simply affirming gratitude is all that is necessary to contact your soul. Expressing gratitude opens the channel. Then comes surrender. This involves nothing less than giving your life to your soul to fulfill its purpose, thereby aligning your personality with your soul. Your ego will resist because it is afraid that it will have to give up its little pleasures, or

Expressing gratitude to the soul creates a connection to the higher dimensions of consciousness.

will have to face up to its fears. However, what the ego fails to understand is that surrender of your little self will help you find your big self. You will also find joy.

Spiritual unfoldment requires that you accept every painful situation as an opportunity for unfoldment. When you continually hide from such opportunities, you set in motion a life threatening situation. It as if the soul is saying , "How can I get your attention? All the bumps and knocks you have taken so far have not raised your awareness to the opportunity for unfoldment in front of you. Perhaps the threat of losing your life will get your attention, so you may finally begin to work on this issue."

Mark Matousek, a journalist with AIDS, writes "the experience of deepened spirituality seems to be nearly universal among those touched by AIDS, although many prefer to clothe their epiphanies in humanist terms. AIDS has actually saved my life, propelling me to change, encouraging me to confront what's difficult, urging my fascination with things divine."[2] Matousek writes that others touched by AIDS have been spurred to explore spirit. "Knowing we may die soon, we've been forced to look toward eternity; to come to treasure what we have." For one of his friends it provided an opportunity to exit from the fast track of life, which he had long grown weary of, and permitted him to spend his days with things he loved most.

This approach to sickness is shared by peoples of other cultures. Kat Duff writes "the traditional Cherokee understands sickness to be a purifying experience intended to return us to our path of destiny and spirit. In shamanic traditions, illness is assumed to have spiritual dimensions."[3]

In *The Healing Power of Illness*, Thorwald Dethlefsen, a spiritual psychologist, and Rüdiger Dahlke, a medical practitioner, suggest that every symptom of sickness offers a challenge and an opportunity to discover the unconscious condition from which it arises.[4] If we do not see the symptoms in these terms, it will continue and intensify. They illustrate the idea of escalation in the following way. Psychological phenomena (thoughts, wishes, fantasies), when not dealt with openly and honestly, become functional disturbances. These in turn lead to acute physical disturbances such as inflammations, wounds and minor accidents. If these do not get your attention of the need for soul attunement, the conditions become chronic. Eventually, the condition becomes incurable or fatal. In your next life you may suffer from congenital deformities or have a severe proclivity to certain diseases. Therefore, even though we come into the world with a new body, we bring with us an old consciousness. Contained in that old consciousness lies all our unresolved unfoldment issues. It is important to recognize that I speak here only of the acceptance of life's context—the situations which we label "chance," but for which the soul is responsible. Acceptance of abuse from others, in any form, should not be part of your life's agenda.

Strategy 8: Focus on relationships

Everything important in life has to do with relationships. Wealth, power and status are valueless without loving relationships. At home or at work, your relationships are the gauges that measure your evolution toward soul consciousness. Only through relationships do we find truth and meaning in our lives and encounter ourselves.

Relationships are the mirrors that tell us who we are. Without such feedback we cannot evolve. Every time we enter into any type of relationship it presents us with an opportunity for unfoldment. Casual encounters, short-term relationships and long-term relationships, all have the same function: they reflect back to us the state of our own consciousness. Whenever you are involved in a painful or discom-

> *It is only through relationships that we find truth and meaning in our lives and encounter ourselves.*

forting relationship, you are encountering a painful aspect of your own consciousness. Behind the pain lies a fear of not being loved and a belief in separation. The pain and discomfort are the results of the lack of attunement of your personality with your soul.

Whenever you feel discomfort in a relationship, be thankful. You have discovered an aspect of your consciousness that needs work. It is an opportunity for you to unfold and grow closer to your soul. Grasp this opportunity by mentally or verbally thanking the person that you believe is causing you discomfort for being in your life. They are not causing your discomfort, your belief about them causes you pain. We are never hurt by others. We are hurt only by the interpretation and meaning that we give to their words and actions.

When people attack you verbally, they are hurting. Every attack is based on fear and a belief in separation. If you respond to an attack by being defensive or retaliating, you have confirmed the reality of the fear of the one attacking. You have bought into the illusion of separation. The only way to deal with attacks is to respond with love. Allow the emotionally laden words to pass by. Do not react to them, but simply respond in a loving way. Listen carefully to what is being said and look for the fear belief behind the words. This is the real issue which needs to be addressed. Remember, however, it is not your place to change the other person; you can change only yourself. If you respond to an attack by being defensive or retaliating, you have work to do on your beliefs. The key to improving relationships is always to work on yourself.

Strategy 9: Forgiveness and honesty

Forgiveness and honesty are fundamental strategies for the attainment of unity consciousness. An unforgiving nature not only promotes separation, but denies your responsibility for creating, or attracting, the circumstances in the first place. This is also dishonest. If there is anyone in your life you cannot forgive, you are stuck in the three-dimensional belief of separation. You have separated yourself from the person you cannot forgive. This is a bitter and painful feeling and almost always self inflicted. The bitterness you feel reflects the lack of alignment between your personality and your soul. You believe that someone wronged you and should be punished. You ignore your role and do not accept any responsibility in the situation. You want all the blame to be put on them because your ego cannot accept the pain and guilt of its separation from the soul. Guilt is about the misalignment of your personality with your soul. When you blame others and make moral judgments about them, you project onto others the issues you are dealing with in your own life. All pain and anger reflect your own misalignment. You are never angry for the reason you think. The following example helps illustrate this point.

John, a partner in an engineering firm, told me he was feeling less tolerant as he approached midlife. He went on to recount that his staff are shoddy performers. "People nowadays do not have the pride in their work that they used to." He was fed up with second-rate work. "What do you do about these situations?" I asked him. "Nothing," he replies. "I finish doing it myself. I don't want to go around axing all the staff." John resented having to do his subordinates' work and justified not doing anything about the situation because axing all the staff would be ludicrous. He also knew in his unconscious mind that axing staff would not change anything.

So I asked John if he had considered a middle path that would involve explaining to the staff that their work needs improvement, showing them how it can be improved, and asking them to redo it. His answer was "No." "Why?" I asked. After a long pause, John admitted he cannot be honest with people. Afraid of telling them something that might hurt their feelings, he is dishonest with them and himself. His personality is out of alignment with his soul because he fears telling people what he really thinks. This fear creates separation. So he projects onto them the guilt he feels about his misalignment. He does this through his angry judgments. What John did not realize was that by continuing down this path of internal disharmony, he was gradually destroying his relationships with staff. By not confronting his staff, he was approaching the point where he would have to fire them. By doing this, they would become sacrifices to his ego which in turn would deepen the disharmony within his soul.

In this example, we see how John's external experience projected inner disharmony. On the surface, the disharmony resulted from a fear of hurting people's feelings. What John really feared were the consequences to himself of telling people how he felt about their work. The question in John's mind was how to deal with the conflict that would ensue if he told the truth. He was so frightened that he preferred not to deal with it. This manner of reaction was something John had learned in his childhood. By blaming his staff and doing the work himself, he did not have to face up to his fears.

John's case is a typical example of the importance of honesty to ourselves. We all have faced similar situations with our colleagues, peers, parents, friends, siblings, and spouses. The lesson that emerges from John's experience is that by not speaking up, John was creating what he feared most.

In *The Ten Natural Laws of Successful Time and Life Management*, Hyrum W. Smith provides a formula for dealing with such situations. He suggests a four-point plan.[5] Begin the conversation by telling the other person, "I have a problem." Give a nonjudgmental and non-threatening description of your perception of the problem. Tell them how the situation makes you feel. Then let the realities of the situation help to produce a change.

At this point, encourage the other person to tell you how he or she feel about the situation. Listen very closely. Their perspective is their reality, just as your perspective is your own reality. Neither perspective may be the truth. You need to reach an understanding of each other's perspective.

If this strategy does not work, there are two questions you need to ask the other person. "If you continue this behavior, knowing full well how I feel about it, do you think it will make our relationship better or worse?" The second question should be, "Do you want our relationship to be better or worse?" This is the ultimate question. If the answer is "better," then the dialogue is still open. If the answer is "worse," then say farewell, and leave without harboring negative energy in your mind.

In such situations, the golden rule is to recognize that other people are on a soul journey just as you are. They are also trying to learn their lessons. If they cannot come to an understanding with you, it is because their fears are too great. They are doing the best they can; but even so, they are finding it impossible to be honest with themselves. Such a person is someone to be understood rather than hated. By forgiving the person, you release the pain inside you. You immediately feel better and more connected. Forgiveness is always an act of self-love and a reconnection to the belief in unity consciousness. Like love, forgiveness must be unconditional. Conditional forgiveness maintains separation and is futile.

Strategy 10: You can change your life
The awareness that comes with the dual discovery that beliefs create your reality and the energy you give out returns to you, opens up the possibility for positive changes in your life. Understanding the mechanism allows you to create a different reality. The techniques for doing this are described below.

Beliefs can be changed by changing your thought patterns. This involves literally taking control of your mind and reprogramming it.

The reprogramming begins when we decide to choose a different way of responding to life situations. In *Empowerment: The art of creating your life the way you want it,* David Gershon and Gail Straub describe a process that can be applied to almost anything that you want to change about yourself.[6]

Affirm what you want.   Step 1: *Determine the particular area of your life that needs change.* Write a statement describing what you deeply desire. Do not feel constrained by your present circumstances. It should reflect what you aspire to achieve. This is the beginning of the new belief you are creating. Write it in the form of an affirmation. It should be positive, specific, succinct, and about you. For the affirmation to be successful, it must be believable by you. If not, reword the affirmation. This is important because, if your affirmation is not believable, it will not create what you want. Affirmations beyond our capacity to believe have no effect on our lives. Similarly, affirmations too readily believable do not take us where we want to go. We need an affirmation at the very edge of what is believable. Gershon and Straub call this the "growing edge" where you are unfolding and where you are experiencing new growth. Your new belief has to become more powerful than your old belief if it is to change your reality. When you have crafted your affirmation, say it aloud to yourself repeatedly. Understand that, as you begin to work with your affirmation, you will bring to the surface all the reasons why what you want to achieve is not possible. Limiting beliefs will sprout like weeds. Reasons why you believe you cannot achieve your vision will flood into your mind from the unconscious. You must bring these beliefs into consciousness and release them if you want to manifest your vision. The story of Jenny illustrates this point.

When Jenny came to see me, she had just become engaged to Paul. She had been married previously, but divorced after six years. Jenny loved Paul and wanted to make sure that this marriage would be a success. However, as her relationship with Paul intensified, she found herself sabotaging the relationship. She could not fully open herself to his love because she felt he would abandon her. The stronger she hung onto the vision of being happily married to Paul, the more she found herself sabotaging the relationship. The cause of this dysfunction was a belief she had learned when her father abandoned her mother and her at the age of six. Now, whenever she had a close relationship with a male, her unconscious fear of abandonment caused her to become defensive. We released the emotion around this belief by emotionally returning to her childhood and reliving the experience of abandonment. Bringing these old feelings into consciousness was all that was needed for Jenny to overcome this belief and begin behaving toward Paul in a different way.

Visualize what you want. Step 2 requires you to *build a mental picture of what you want to create in your life.* This vision will reinforce your affirmation. Make the image evocative. Give it the feeling that you want to feel. Make just one powerful image that includes all aspects of the situation you would like to create. The more focused and evocative the image, the more powerful it becomes. Make sure you are in the image. See yourself enjoying the situation and getting what you want from it. Your image can be literal, or a metaphor. Lastly, draw the image you have created. Do it in any medium you choose. Do not worry if you have no drawing skills or are color blind. Simply get an image down on paper so you can see it. By making it visible you are already beginning the process of making it concrete.

The vision has another important role to play. Wherever you put your thought, that is where your energy goes. If you focus on your problem, you make it more real. The problem assumes greater proportions as you pump your thought energy into it. If, instead of putting your thought energy into your problem, you put it into your vision, you help to manifest what you want to create. This technique is used in the martial arts to break wooden beams with a blow of the hand, and by fire walkers to walk across burning coals with bare feet. By focusing your attention on the other side of the beam, rather on the problem (the beam) you are able to move your hand easily through the obstruction. Similarly, the fire walker thinks only about being on the other side of the fire, never about the burning coals that lie on the path.

Grow the future. Step 3 is to *create the conditions in which your seed (the affirmation) can become your vision (your image)*. The seed will not grow unless it is nurtured. Nurturing involves looking at your image and repeating your affirmation daily. Keep your vision in mind with confident expectation. The more energy you focus on your vision, the more easily it will manifest. Fear and worry serve only to obstruct the process.

Energize your vision. Step 4 is to *energize your vision*. You do this through the power of your intent. Talk, think, and plan as if your vision is going to be reality. Tell people about it. Take whatever steps are necessary to put in motion what you want to achieve. All visions manifest through confident expectation of the result. By creating a vision of how you would like your life to be, and crafting affirmations that support the vision, you unleash the forces of creation that exist in the higher levels of consciousness. From a three-dimensional perspective, your life will appear to be full of strange and fortuitous coincidences. From a higher perspective, you will be working with the universal principles by which we manifest reality. You manifested your present life unconsciously. The trick is to now do it purposefully.

As you start to manifest what you want in life, you begin to feel your personal power. You also begin to recognize that through the conscientious application of empowerment techniques, you have the ability to respond to any situation that might arise in your life. You will never again be a victim. What you learn about creating reality as you prepare your affirmation and craft your vision, the soul already knows. This is the normal way of creation in the fourth-dimension of consciousness. You create your vision in your mind, focus your intention, and energize it with your will. These techniques assist greatly in the unfoldment process, but are at their most powerful when you align your vision with your soul's purpose. When you do this, you truly create a life for your soul.

The human race is in the midst of making an evolutionary leap. Whether or not we succeed in that leap is your personal responsibility. Scott Peck

In today's highly interdependent world, individuals and nations can no longer resolve many of their problems by themselves. We need one another. We must therefore develop a sense of individual responsibility . . . It is our collective and individual responsibility to protect and nurture the global family, to support its weaker members, and to preserve and tend to the environment in which we all live. The Dalai Lama

I don't know what your destiny will be, but one thing I do know; the only ones among you who will be really happy are those who have sought and found how to serve. Albert Schweitzer

The real, the great period of human fulfillment on planet earth, is only now about to begin. Robert Muller

12

Living Your Life as a Soul

The life you are now living is a gift from your soul. You would not be on earth if your soul had not chosen to manifest in three-dimensional consciousness. The personality that lives in three-dimensional consciousness is able to experience higher levels of consciousness. The transition from three-dimensional consciousness to soul consciousness simply involves a shift in awareness. Within the framework of three-dimensional consciousness, your soul has given your personality freedom of choice. In matters that go beyond three-dimensional consciousness, such as birth and death, the soul is in charge.

The most important decision you can make as a personality is to align yourself with your soul. As you begin to accept and identify with your multidimensional reality, you recognize within yourself the powers of creation and communication that exist in the higher dimensions of consciousness. You become increasingly sensitive to the energy that permeates and surrounds all living things. You begin to understand and know things that are beyond your current knowledge. You rely less on logic and more on intuition, and your words reflect the wisdom of your soul.

You may find that you develop other gifts—the ability to heal disease, the ability to see auras, and the ability to communicate with soul entities not living in three-dimensional consciousness. All these abilities are simply a reflection of your increased awareness to the higher dimensions of consciousness.

By aligning yourself with your soul, you are also able to raise the natural frequency of your energy vibration. Your outlook becomes more positive and you begin to experience longer periods of joy and peace. As a personality, you have much to gain by aligning with your soul.

Throughout history there have been examples of men and women who have lived in higher states of consciousness. In 1902, Richard Maurice Bucke published his classic work *Cosmic Consciousness*[1] and posited that the number of individuals living in cosmic consciousness has been increasing over the past 2,000 years. He considered such people the outposts of human evolution, providing an example of where the human race is heading. Bucke describes cosmic consciousness as a consciousness of the cosmos, of life itself and the order of the universe, accompanied by a feeling of elevation, elation and joy, a quickening of the moral sense, and a consciousness of eternal life.

> Just as, long ago, self-consciousness appeared in the best specimens of our ancestral race in the prime of life, and gradually became more and more universal and appeared in the individual at an earlier and earlier age, . . . so will cosmic consciousness become more and more universal and appear earlier in the individual life until the race at large will possess this faculty. The same race and not the same; for a cosmic consciousness race will not be the race which exists today, any more than the present race of men is the same race which existed prior to the evolution of self-consciousness. The simple truth is there has lived on earth, "appearing at intervals," for thousands of years among ordinary men, the first faint beginnings of another race; walking the earth and breathing the air with us, but at the same time walking another earth and breathing another air of which we know little or nothing, but which is, all the same, our spiritual life, as its absence would be our spiritual death. This new race is in act of being born from us, and in the near future it will occupy and possess the earth.[2]

We are now in the age of transition toward this "new race" defined by Bucke. Spiritual unfoldment is accelerating at an unprecedented pace. The reality of the vision of a world inhabited by humans living in soul consciousness is close at hand. Many will unfold into cosmic consciousness. It will take but a few generations for the presence of the new race to become obvious to all. The first members of the new race are manifesting as world servers. They actively care for the earth and humanity. In their service, they reflect the principles of unity consciousness. From among them will emerge a new group of leaders who will bring new insights and wisdom. They will question and challenge the entrenched belief systems and power structures of our age. This "new race" will understand that the survival of the human species depends on the acceptance of values that support unity consciousness. Every individual on the planet is a potential world server. Every one of us has a gift to offer and a role to perform in the new world order. If you are not living your life in harmony with your soul, or offering your gift to humanity, now is the time to unfold.

Appendix

The process of liberating your soul can be accelerated through daily meditation. As you connect with your inner self, you move into the higher dimensions of consciousness. Spending time in these higher dimensions helps to release the fears that cause stress and can produce all-round health benefits. I have put together four meditations designed specifically to accelerate spiritual unfoldment. The first two focus on the process—releasing fears and manifesting vision. The second two focus on the result—experiencing soul and unity consciousness. The boxed set of two tapes can be obtained by filling in the order form at the end of this book.

Releasing Your Fears (*The Flower*)

This meditation can be used whenever you feel anxiety or emotional discomfort. It dissipates the fears that are causing you distress. In the meditation, you become a flower that is gently unfolding. As each petal unfolds in the bright light of the sun, fears are released. Gradually, the sun calls you to release all your fears, until the flower is in full bloom, with its beauty visible to the whole world. The open flower is your soul. When you are free from fear, you will be able to live in soul consciousness. This meditation is particularly useful for healing relationships and releasing the limiting beliefs preventing you from manifesting your vision.

Empowering Your Vision (*The Theater*)

Preparing for this meditation is extremely important. The more preparation you do, the more powerful will be the result. The surest way to overcome any problem is to focus on how you want things to be. Before listening to this meditation, spend several hours working on your vision. Make it positive, succinct, specific, magnetic, and say it as if it already exists. It must be about yourself, not others, and it should be in the realms of what you consider believable. When you have written down your thoughts, draw a picture of your vision with you in it. Make it as detailed as you wish. In this meditation you act out your vision on the stage of a theater. The acting out of the vision energizes it and helps build your confidence. This meditation is particularly effective when used in combination with *The Flower*.

Identifying With Your Soul (*Soul Consciousness*)

This meditation assists you in identifying with your soul. The meditation was created by Roberto Assagioli, an Italian transpersonal psychotherapist who recognized that many of the problems we encounter in our lives are due to the splitting of the personality from the soul. As you identify with your soul, the personality merges into soul consciousness and you embark on a journey of self-realization. During this meditation, you disidentify with the physical, emotional, and mental "you," and identify with the source of your "being." You become a soul having a human experience. This meditation assists you in gaining a broader but more centered perspective on life. It can and should be used frequently.

Journeying into Unity (*Unity Consciousness*)

This meditation helps you expand the boundaries of your identity to connect with other souls and all creation. It leads you progressively into higher states of awareness until you become one with all there is. This meditation is particularly useful when you are feeling discord, isolated, or lonely. It reconnects you with your family, colleagues, community, nature, and the universe. It gives you a feeling of oneness and a profound sense of peace and connection.

References

Chapter 2: The Consciousness Model

1. P.D. Ouspensky, *Tertium Organum: A key to the mysteries of the world*, New York: Vintage Books, March 1982, pp. 262-263.

2. F. Kapra, *The Tao of Physics: An explanation of the parallels between modern physics and Eastern mysticism*, London: Fontana Paperbacks, 1983, p. 155.

3. P.C.W. Davies, *The Mind-Body Problem and Quantum Theory*, *Proceedings of the Symposium on Consciousness and Survival*, Ed. J.S. Spring, Sausalito, California: Institute of Noetic Sciences, 1987, pp. 113-114.

4. M. Talbot, *The Holographic Universe*, New York: Harper Collins, 1991, p. 50.

5. N. Friedman, *Bridging Science and Spirit*, St. Louis: Living Lake Books, 1994, p. 292.

6. W. James, *The Varieties of Religious Experience*, New York: Penguin Classics, 1985, p. xxi.

7. Ibid., pp. 408-409.

8. Ibid., p. 410.

9. Ibid., p. 6.

10. C.G. Jung, *The Portable Jung*, Ed. J. Campbell, Harmondsworth: Penguin Books, 1980, p. 466.

11. Ibid., p. 468.

12. J. Hardy, *A Psychology with a Soul: Psychosynthesis in evolutionary context*, Arkana: London, 1987.

13. *Spiritual Emergencies: When personal transformation becomes a crisis*, Eds. S. Grof and C. Grof, Jeremy P. Tarcher: Los Angeles, 1990.

14. S.C. Roberts, *Multiple Realities*, Common Boundary, May/June 1992, pp. 24-31.

15. Ibid.

16. Ibid.

17. G. Zukav, *The Seat of the Soul*, New York: Fireside, 1990.

Chapter 3: The Fourth Dimension of Consciousness
1. R.W. Clark, *Einstein the Life and Times*, New York: World Publishing Co., 1971, p. 159.
2. A. Hastings, *With the Tongues of Men and Angels: A study of channeling*, Ted Buchholz: Orlando, 1990.
3. B.A. Brennan, *Hands of Light: A guide to healing through the human energy field*, New York: Bantam Books, 1988, pp. 41-56.
4. M. Talbot, *The Holographic Universe*, New York: Harper Collins, 1991, p. 176.

Chapter 4: Who Am I?
1. K. Lashley, *In Search of the Engram in Physiological Mechanisms in Animal Behavior*, New York: Academic Press, 1950, pp. 454-82.
2. M. Talbot, *The Holographic Universe*, New York: Harper Collins, 1991, p. 244.
3. R.A. Moody, *Life After Life*, New York: Bantam Books, 1990.
4. L. Dossey, *Recovering the Soul: A scientific and spiritual search*, New York: Bantam Books, 1989, pp. 92-98.
5. Ibid., pp. 291.
6. D. Bohm, *Unfolding Meaning*, London: Ark Paperbacks, 1987.
7. M. Talbot, *The Holographic Universe*, New York: Harper Collins, 1991, p. 264.
8. R. Assagioli, *Psychosynthesis: A manual of principles and techniques*, Wellingborough: Crucible, 1990, p. 17.
9. R. Assagioli, *The Act of Will*, London: Penguin Books, 1974.
10. A. Maslow, *Towards a Psychology of Being*, Van Nostrand, 1968.

Chapter 5: Why Am I Living This Reality?
1. M. Talbot, *The Holographic Universe*, New York: Harper Collins, 1991, p. 93-94.

Chapter 6: The Origins of Beliefs
1. R.J. Woolger, *Other Lives, Other Selves*: New York: Bantam Books, 1988.
2. Ibid., p. 96
3. I. Stevenson, *Some Questions Related to Cases of Reincarnation Type*, Journal of the American Society for Psychical Research, October 1974, p. 407.

Chapter 7: Liberating the Soul
1. H.D. Johns, *From Fear to Fury: What you need to know about the anger in your life*, Vantage Press: New York, 1990.
2. K. Wilber, *No Boundary: Eastern and Western approaches to personal growth*, Boston: Shambhala Publications, 1981.
3. K. Wilber, *The Spectrum of Consciousness*, Wheaton: The Theosophical Publishing House, 1989.
4. *A Course in Miracles*, Tiburon: Foundation for Inner Peace, 1986.

Chapter 10: Five Pathways to Unity
1. C. G. Jung, *Synchronicity: An acausal connecting principle*, Princeton: Bollingen Paperback Edition, 1973.
2. C. G. Jung and W. Pauli, *The Interpretation and Nature of the Psyche*, New York: Pantheon, 1955.
3. C. G. Jung, *On Synchronicity, Man and his Time*, New York: Eranos Yearbooks, 1957.
4. D.F. Peat, *Synchronicity: The bridge between matter and mind*, New York: Bantam Books, 1987, p. 25.
5. *The Portable Jung*, Ed. J. Campbell, Harmondsworth: Penguin Books, 1980, p. 518.
6. D. Bohm, *Unfolding Meaning*, London: Ark Paperbacks, 1987, p. 12.

Chapter 11: Ten Strategies for Attaining Soul Consciousness
1. N. Branden, *The Six Pillars of Self Esteem*, New York: Bantam Books, 1994.

2. M. Matousek, *Savage Grace*, Common Boundary, May/June 1993, pp. 22-31.

3. K. Duff, *The Alchemy of Illness*, Common Boundary, May/June, 1993. pp. 38-45.

4. T. Dethlefsen and R. Dahlke, *The Healing Power of Illness: The meaning of symptoms and how to interpret them*, Shaftesbury: Element Books Limited, 1990.

5. H.W. Smith, *The 10 Natural Laws of Successful Time and Life Management: Proven strategies for increased productivity and inner peace*, New York: Warner Books, 1994, pp. 163-164.

6. D. Gershon and G. Straub, *Empowerment: The art of creating your life as you want it*, New York: Dell Publishing, 1989.

Chapter 12: Living Your Life as a Soul

1. R. M. Bucke, *Cosmic Consciousness*, New York: E. P. Dutton, 1969.

2. Ibid., pp. 383-384.

Bibliography

Bailey, A.A. *Serving Humanity.* A compilation of the works of Alice Bailey. New York: Lucis Publishing, 1972.

Bianchi, E.G. *Aging as a Spiritual Journey.* New York: Crossroad, 1982.

Becker, E. *The Denial of Death.* New York: The Free Press, 1973.

Chopra, D. *Quantum Healing.* New York: Bantam Books, 1989.

Cerminara, G, *Many Mansions: The Edgar Cacey story.* New York: Signet, 1967.

Davies, P.D. *God and the New Physics.* New York: Touchstone, 1983.

Gerber, R. *Vibrational Medicine: New choices for healing ourselves.* Santa Fe: Bear and Company, 1988.

Kapleau, P. *The Wheel of Life and Death.* New York: Anchor Books, 1989.

MacGregor, G. *Reincarnation in Christianity.* Wheaton: Theosophical Publishing House, 1978.

Moore, T. *Care of the Soul: A guide for creating depth and sacredness in everyday life.* New York: Walker and Company, 1992.

Pagels, E. *The Gnostic Gospels.* New York: Vintage Books, 1979.

Pelletier, K.R. *Mind as Healer. Mind as Slayer.* New York: Dell Publishing, 1977.

Roberts, J. *Seth Speaks.* New York: Bantam Books, 1988.

Roberts, J. *The Nature of Personal Reality.* New York: Bantam Books, 1988.

Sheldrake, R. *A New Science of Life.* Los Angeles: Jeremy P. Tarcher, 1987.

Watson, L. *The Nature of Things: An enquiry into the secret life of inanimate objects.* London: Hodder and Stoughton, 1990.

Zweig, C. and Abrams, J., Eds. *Meeting the Shadow.* Los Angeles: Jeremy P. Tarcher, 1991.

Index

Ordering Information

Price information:
The Book: *A Guide to Liberating Your Soul*
US$ 13.95, CAN$ 18.95, UK£ 9.99, AUS$ 19.95, NZ$ 22.95

The Audio Tapes: *Four Meditations for Liberating Your Soul*
(Box of 2 tapes with instructions). US$ 16.95, CAN$ 23.95,
UK£ 11.99, AUS$ 23.95, NZ$ 27.95

The Video Tapes: Video tapes of Richard Barrett's *Liberating Your Soul* seminars will be available in 1995. If you are interested in purchasing video tapes please tick the "yes" box on the order form.

Shipping information:
Shipping within USA and Canada: US$ 4.50 per book, or box of tapes. US$ 2.50 for additional books, or tapes, to same address. Tapes, free shipping with purchase of book.

Shipping outside USA and Canada: Europe, add 35% to subtotal. Elsewhere, add 45% to subtotal. Surface mail to Europe and elsewhere add 20% to subtotal.

For credit card orders call: 1 (800) 879-4214

Order Form

To order books and tapes, and for information about upcoming video releases, please make a copy this page, fill out the required information, and send your check to:

Fulfilling Books
P.O. Box 19926, Alexandria, VA 22320
Tel: (703) 768-9558 Fax: (703) 768-9560

Please send me the following items. I understand that I may return the book or tapes for a full refund, for any reason.

Items:	Number	Cost
The Book: *A Guide to Liberating Your Soul*		
The Audio Tapes: *Four Meditations for Liberating Your Soul*		
The Video Tapes: *I am interested in receiving information about video tapes.*	Yes: □ No: □	
Subtotal		
Tax 4.5% VA Residents		
Shipping		
TOTAL ENCLOSED		

Your Name: ....
Address: ....
City: .... State & Zip Code: ....
Country: .... Daytime Phone: ....